BIG-DATA
PROCESSING WITH
APACHE SPARK

Srini Penchikala

Big-Data Processing with Apache Spark

Published by C4Media, publisher of InfoQ.com

Production Editor: Ana Ciobotaru

Copyeditor: Laurie Nyveen

Cover and Interior Design: Dragos Balasoiu

Library of Congress Cataloguing-in-Publication Data:

ISBN: 978-1-387-65995-1

Printed in the United States of America

Acknowledgements

First of all, I would like to thank Floyd Marinescu, who gave me the opportunity back in 2007 to join the InfoQ editorial team and contribute to the reader community. It's been a rewarding experience.

I want to thank Charles Humble, editor-in-chief at InfoQ.com, for his guidance and support in writing the article series on Apache Spark and finally writing this mini-book.

Special thanks go to my colleagues Alex Giamas, Dylan Raithel, and Alexandre Rodrigues of the Data Science editorial team at InfoQ for review and feedback on the content.

I would like to also thank my wife Kavitha and my daughter Srihasa for their continued support and patience during the writing of this book.

About the Author

//

Srini Penchikala currently works as Senior Software Architect in Austin, Texas. He is also the Lead Editor of Data Science community at InfoQ. Srini has over 22 years of experience in software architecture, design and development. He is the co-author of "Spring Roo in Action" book from Manning Publications. Srini has presented at conferences like Big Data Conference, Enterprise Data World, JavaOne, SEI Architecture Technology Conference (SATURN), IT Architect Conference (ITARC), No Fluff Just Stuff, NoSQL Now and Project World Conference. He also published several articles on software architecture, security and risk management, and NoSQL databases on websites like InfoQ, The ServerSide, OReilly Network (ONJava), DevX Java, java.net and JavaWorld.

Dedication

This book is dedicated to my parents, Venkata Siva Reddy and Lakshmi.

Contents

Preface

//////////////////////

Apache Spark is an open-source big-data processing framework built around speed, ease of use, and sophisticated analytics.

Spark has several advantages compared to other big-data and MapReduce technologies like Hadoop and Storm. It provides a comprehensive, unified framework with which to manage big-data processing requirements for datasets that are diverse in nature (text data, graph data, etc.) and that come from a variety of sources (batch versus real-time streaming data).

Spark enables applications in HDFS clusters to run up to a hundred times faster in memory and ten times faster even when running on disk.

In this mini-book, the reader will learn about the Apache Spark framework and will develop Spark programs for use cases in big-data analysis. The book covers all the libraries that are part of Spark ecosystem, which includes Spark Core, Spark SQL, Spark Streaming, Spark MLlib, and Spark GraphX.

What is in an InfoQ mini-book?

InfoQ mini-books are designed to be concise, intending to serve technical architects looking to get a firm conceptual understanding of a new technology or technique in a quick yet in-depth fashion. You can think of these books as covering a topic strategically or essentially. After reading a mini-book, the reader should have a fundamental understanding of a technology, including when and where to apply it, how it relates to other technologies, and an overall feeling that they have assimilated the combined knowledge of other professionals who have already figured out what this technology is about. The reader will then be able to make intelligent decisions about the technology once their projects require it, and can delve into sources of more detailed information (such as larger books or tutorials) at that time.

Who this book is for

This mini-book intends to provide an accelerated introduction to big-data processing with Apache Spark. Some programming experience and prior knowledge of the Java Virtual Machine (JVM) is useful but not essential. No prior knowledge of big data or Spark is assumed, but readers entirely new to the field may first want to read the *Getting a Handle on Big Data* eMag, also from InfoQ, to get a quick overview of the topic.

What you need for this book

You'll need the following software in your local development environment to be able to run the Spark programs discussed in this book:

1. JDK 8,
2. Apache Spark, and
3. VMware or Virtual Box (if you want to run Spark in a VM environment).

The code examples discussed in this book will be available at the following Github project:

https://github.com/spenchikala/big-data-processing-spark-mini-book

Readers are encouraged to check out the website from time to time to get the latest version of the code as the newer versions of frameworks like Apache Spark and Kafka may force some code changes in the sample application.

Conventions

We use a number of typographical conventions within this book that distinguish between different kinds of information.

Code in the text, including database table names, folder names, file extensions, path names, dummy URLs, user input, and Twitter handles are shown as follows:

"The size of the Java heap can be typically controlled by two flags, `-Xms` for the initial size and `-Xmx` for the maximum size."

A block of code is set out as follows:

```
public class GCInformation {

    public static void main(String[] args) {

        List<GarbageCollectorMXBean> gcMxBeans =
```

```
                ManagementFactory.getGarbageCollectorMX
Beans();

        for (GarbageCollectorMXBean gcMxBean : gcMx
Beans) {
            System.out.println(gcMxBean.getName());
        }
    }
}
```

When we want to draw attention to a particular part of the code, it is highlighted in bold:

```
[PSYoungGen: 542688K->253792K(628224K)]
1290819K->1185723K(1629184K), 0.3456630 secs] [Times:
user=1.01 sys=0.08, real=0.35 secs]
2015-03-07T22:11:25.540+0000: 7.239: [Full GC
[PSYoungGen: 253792K->0K(628224K)] [ParOldGen:
931931K->994693K(1595392K)] 1185723K->994693K(2223616K)
[PSPermGen: 3015K->3015K(21504K)], 3.1400810 secs]
[Times: user=8.78 sys=0.15, real=3.14 secs]
```

Reader feedback

We always welcome feedback from our readers. Let us know what you think about this book — what you liked or disliked. Reader feedback helps us develop titles that you get the most out of.

To send us feedback, e-mail us at feedback@infoq.com.

If you have expertise in a topic and you are interested in either writing about it or contributing to a book about it, please take a look at our mini-book guidelines at http://www.infoq.com/minibook-guidelines.

PART ONE

Overview

What is Spark?

Apache Spark is an open-source unified big-data processing framework built around speed, ease of use, and sophisticated analytics. It was originally developed in 2009 in UC Berkeley's AMPLab, and open-sourced in 2010 as an Apache project.

Spark has several advantages compared to other big-data and MapReduce technologies like Hadoop, Storm, and Mahout.

First of all, Spark provides a comprehensive, unified framework with which to manage big-data processing requirements for datasets that are diverse in nature (text data, images, video content, graph data, etc.) and that come from a variety of sources (online web application data, batch versus real-time streaming data).

It enables applications in Hadoop clusters to run up to a hundred times faster in memory and ten times faster even when running on disk.

Spark lets us quickly write applications in Java, Scala, or Python. It comes with a built-in set of over 80 high-level operators. And we can use it interactively to query data within the shell.

In addition to `Map` and `Reduce` operations, it supports SQL queries, streaming data, machine learning and graph-data processing. Developers can use these capabilities alone or combine them to run in a single data pipeline use case.

This first part of this mini-book will look at what Spark is, how it compares with a typical MapReduce solution, and how it provides a complete suite of tools for big-data processing.

Hadoop and Spark

Hadoop has been around for 10 years as a big-data processing technology and has proven to be the solution of choice for processing large datasets. MapReduce is a great solution for one-pass computations but is not efficient for use cases that require multi-pass computations and algorithms. Each step in the data-processing workflow has one map phase and one reduce phase and we'll need to convert any use case to a MapReduce pattern to use this solution.

The job output data between each step has to be stored in the distributed file system before the next step can begin, and replication and disk storage tend to slow this approach. Also, Hadoop solutions typically include clusters that are hard to set up and manage. Hadoop also requires the integration of several tools for different big-data use cases (like Mahout for machine learning and Storm for streaming-data processing).

If we wanted to do something complicated, we would have had to string together a series of MapReduce jobs and execute them in sequence. Each of those jobs has high latency, and none could start until the previous job had finished completely.

Spark allows programmers to develop complex, multistep data pipelines using the directed acyclic graph (DAG) pattern. It also supports in-memory data sharing across DAGs, so that different jobs can work with the same data without having to re-compute the data for every step.

Spark runs on top of existing Hadoop Distributed File System (HDFS) infrastructure to provide additional functionality. It provides support for deploying Spark applications in an existing Hadoop v1 cluster (with SIMR: Spark Inside MapReduce), Hadoop v2 YARN cluster, or even Apache Mesos.

We should look at Spark as an alternative to Hadoop MapReduce for new applications if we are already using Hadoop in our organization, rather than to completely replace Hadoop. Spark is intended not to replace Hadoop but to provide a comprehensive and unified solution to manage different big-data requirements and use cases.

Spark features

Spark enhances MapReduce with less expensive shuffles in data processing. With capabilities like in-memory data storage and near-real-time processing, it can run several times faster than other big-data technologies.

Spark also supports lazy evaluation of big-data queries, which helps with optimization of the steps in data-processing workflows. It provides a higher-level API to improve developer productivity and a consistent architecture for big-data solutions.

Spark holds intermediate results in memory rather than writing them to disk, which is efficient especially when we need to work on the same dataset multiple times. It's designed to be an execution engine that works both in memory and on disk. Spark operators perform external operations when data does not fit in memory. Spark can be used for processing datasets that exceed the aggregate memory in a cluster.

Spark will attempt to store as much data in memory as possible and then will spill to disk. It can store part of a dataset in memory and the remaining data on the disk. We have to look at our data and use cases to assess the memory requirements. With this in-memory data storage, Spark comes with a performance advantage.

Other Spark features include:

- support for more than just map and reduce functions;
- optimization of arbitrary operator graphs;
- lazy evaluation of big-data queries, which helps optimize the overall data-processing workflow;
- concise and consistent APIs in Scala, Java, and Python programming languages; and
- an interactive shell for Scala and Python (not available in Java prior to version 1.9).

Spark is written in the Scala programming language and runs on the JVM. It currently supports the following languages for developing applications:

- Scala,
- Java,
- Python,
- Clojure, and
- R.

Spark ecosystem

In addition to the Spark Core API, other libraries are part of the Spark ecosystem and provide additional capabilities in big-data analysis and machine learning.

These libraries include the following:

- Spark Streaming can be used to process real-time streaming data. This is based on the micro-batch style of computing and processing. It uses the DStream, which is basically a series of RDDs, to process the real-time data. (We'll look at what RDDs are a little bit later in this discussion).

- Spark SQL can expose the Spark datasets over the JDBC API and allow running SQL-like queries on Spark data with traditional BI and visualization tools. Spark SQL allows users to extract their data from different formats (like JSON, Parquet, or a database), transform it, and expose it for ad-hoc querying.

- Spark MLlib is Spark's scalable machine-learning library. It consists of common learning algorithms and utilities, including classification, regression, clustering, collaborative filtering, dimensionality reduction, and underlying optimization primitives.

- Spark GraphX is the Spark API for graphs and graph-parallel computation. At a high level, GraphX extends the Spark RDD by introducing the resilient distributed property graph: a directed multi-graph with properties attached to each vertex and edge. To support graph computation, GraphX exposes a set of fundamental operators (for example, `subgraph`, `joinVertices`, and `aggregateMessages`) and an optimized variant of the Pregel API. In addition, GraphX includes a growing collection of graph algorithms and builders to simplify graph analysis.

Outside of these libraries, there are other frameworks like Alluxio that integrate nicely with Spark.

Alluxio (formerly known as Tachyon) is a memory-centric distributed file system that enables reliable file sharing at memory speed across cluster frameworks such as Spark and MapReduce. It caches working-set files in memory, thereby avoiding going to disk to load frequently read datasets. This allows different jobs/queries and frameworks to access cached files at memory speed.

BlinkDB is an approximate-query engine to use for running interactive SQL queries on large volumes of data. It allows users to trade off query accuracy for response time. It works on large datasets by running queries on data samples and presenting results annotated with meaningful error bars. BlinkDB's later versions are being maintained under a new project called iOLAP.

There are also adapters for integration with other products like Cassandra (Spark Cassandra Connector) and R (SparkR). Cassandra Connector lets us use Spark to access data stored in a Cassandra database and perform data analytics on that data.

Figure 1.1 shows how these different libraries in the Spark ecosystem are related.

Spark Framework Ecosystem

BlinkDB					
Spark SQL	Spark Streaming	Machine Learning (Mllib)	Graph Analytics (GraphX)	Spark Cassandra Connector	Spark R Integration
Spark Core					

Figure 1.1. Spark framework libraries.

We'll explore these libraries later in the book.

Spark architecture

Spark's architecture includes three main components:

- data storage,
- API, and
- management framework.

Data storage: Spark uses the HDFS file system for data storage. It works with any Hadoop-compatible data source including HDFS, HBase, Cassandra, etc.

API: The API allows application developers to create Spark-based applications with a standard interface. Spark provides APIs for the Scala, Java, Python, and R programming languages.

Resource management: Spark can be deployed as a stand-alone server or on a distributed computing framework like Mesos or YARN.

Figure 1.2 models these components of the Spark architecture.

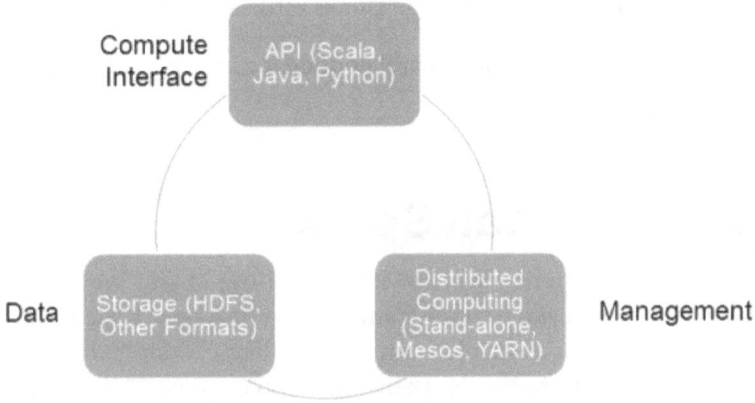

Figure 1.2. Spark architecture.

Resilient distributed datasets

The resilient distributed dataset (RDD) — based on "Resilient Distributed Datasets: A Fault-Tolerant Abstraction for In-Memory Cluster Computing" (Matei et al 2012) — is the core concept of the Spark framework. Think of RDD as a table in a database, which can hold any type of data. Spark stores data in RDDs on different partitions.

RDDs help with rearranging the computations and optimizing the data processing. They are also fault tolerant because the RDD knows how to recreate and re-compute the datasets.

RDDs are immutable. We can modify a RDD with a transformation operation but the transformation returns a new RDD while the original RDD remains the same.

RDD supports two types of operations: transformations and actions.

Transformations don't return a single value but return a new RDD. Nothing gets evaluated when you call a transformation function; it just takes the original RDD and returns a new RDD. Some of the transformation functions are: map, filter, flatMap, groupByKey, reduceByKey, aggregateByKey, pipe, and coalesce.

Action operations evaluate and return a new value. When an action function is called on a RDD object, all the data-processing queries are computed at that time and the resulting value is returned.

Some of the action operations are: reduce, collect, count, first, take, countByKey, and foreach.

How to install Spark

There are few different ways to install and use Spark. We can install it on a machine as a stand-alone framework or use one of the Spark virtual-machine images available from vendors like Cloudera, Hortonworks, or MapR. We can also use Spark installed and configured in the cloud (for example, on Databricks Community Edition).

We'll install Spark as a stand-alone framework and launch it locally. Spark 2.1.0 was released at the end of 2016. We'll use this version to demonstrate application code.

How to run Spark

When we install Spark on a local machine or use a cloud-based installation, we can use a few different modes to connect to the Spark engine. The following table shows the master URL parameters for the different modes of running Spark.

Master URL	Description
Local	Run Spark locally with one worker thread (i.e. no parallelism at all).
local[K]	Run Spark locally with K worker threads (ideally, set this to the number of cores on your machine).
local[*]	Run Spark locally with as many worker threads as logical cores on your machine.
spark://HOST:PORT	Connect to the given Spark standalone cluster master. The port must be whichever one your master is configured to use, which is 7077 by default.
mesos://HOST:PORT	Connect to the given Mesos cluster. The port must be whichever one your is configured to use, which is 5050 by default. Or, for a Mesos cluster using ZooKeeper, use mesos://zk://....
yarn-client	Connect to a YARN cluster in client mode. The cluster location will be found based on the HADOOP_CONF_DIR variable.
yarn-cluster	Connect to a YARN cluster in cluster mode. The cluster location will be found based on HADOOP_CONF_DIR.

Table 1.1. A Spark cluster's master URL's configuration options.

How to interact with Spark

Once Spark is up and running, we can connect to it using the Spark shell for interactive data analysis. The Spark shell is available in the Scala and Python languages. Java did not support an interactive shell previously, but it is available in JDK 9. The REPL (read-eval-print loop) tool in Java is called JShell.

You use the commands `spark-shell.cmd` and `pyspark.cmd` to run the Spark shell using Scala and Python languages respectively.

Spark web console

When Spark is running in any mode, you can view its job results and other statistics by accessing its web console at the URL: `http://localhost:4040`

The Spark console is shown in Figure 1.3. It has tabs for Stages, Storage, Environment, and Executors.

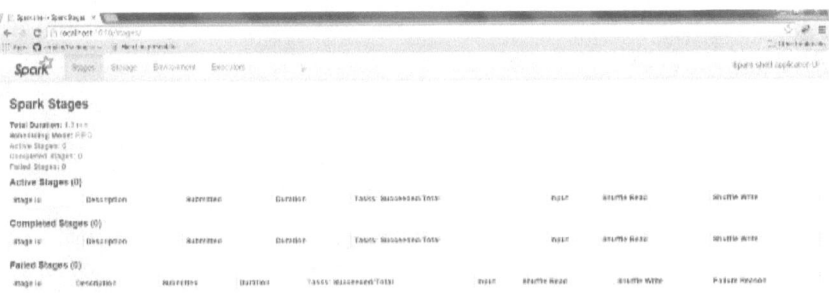

Figure 1.3. The Spark web console.

Shared variables

Spark provides two types of shared variables to make it efficient to run the Spark programs in a cluster. These are broadcast variables and accumulators.

Broadcast variables allow developers to keep read-only variables cached on each machine instead of sending a copy of it with tasks. They can be used to more efficiently give copies of large-input datasets to the nodes in the cluster.

The following Scala code snippet shows how to use the broadcast variables.

```
//
// Broadcast Variables
//
val broadcastVar = sc.broadcast(Array(1, 2, 3))
broadcastVar.value
```

Accumulators are only added using an associative operation and can therefore be efficiently supported in parallel. They can be used to implement counters (as in MapReduce) or sums. Tasks running on the cluster can add to an accumulator variable using the add method. However, they cannot read its value. Only the driver program can read the accumulator's value.

The code snippet below shows how to use an accumulator shared variable.

```
//
// Accumulators
//

val accum = sc.accumulator(0, "My Accumulator")

sc.parallelize(Array(1, 2, 3, 4)).foreach(x => accum +=
x)

accum.value
```

Sample Spark application

The sample application in this section is a simple application for counting words. This is the same example used to teach big-data processing with Hadoop. We'll perform some data analysis on a text file to count how many words are in the file and how many times they repeat. The text file and the dataset in this example are small, but the same Spark programs can be used for large datasets without any code modifications. Similar to Hadoop, the Spark run-time environment will automatically distribute the data to different nodes in the cluster for faster data processing.

To keep the discussion simple, we'll use the Spark Scala shell.

First, let's install Spark on our local machine. We will need Java Development Kit (JDK) installed for Spark to work locally. This is covered in the first step below.

We will also need to install Spark software on our machine. The instructions on how to do this are covered in step II.

Note: These instructions are for a Windows environment. To use a different operating system (Linux or macOS), we would need to modify the system variables and directory paths to match it.

I. INSTALL JDK

Download the JDK from the Oracle website. JDK 8 is recommended.

Install JDK in a directory with a name that does not include spaces, meaning install it in a new directory called something like "`c:\dev`", not in "`c:\Program Files`". "`Program Files`" has a space in the directory name, which causes issues when we run Spark programs.

After installation, verify that JDK installed correctly by navigating to the "bin" folder in the JDK directory and typing the following command:

```
java -version
```

If JDK is correctly installed, the above command will display the Java version number.

II. INSTALL SPARK

Download the latest version of Spark from the Spark website (the latest version at the time of writing is Spark 2.2.0). You can choose a specific Spark installation depending on the Hadoop version. I downloaded Spark for Hadoop 2.7 or later, called spark-2.2.0-bin-hadoop2.7.tgz.

Unzip the installation file to a local directory (for example, `c:\dev`).

To verify the Spark installation, navigate to the Spark directory and launch the Spark shell using the following commands.

For Windows:

```
c:
cd c:\dev\spark-2.2.0-bin-hadoop2.7
bin\spark-shell
```

For macOS/Linux:

```
cd /home/m1/workspace/spark-2.2.0-bin-hadoop2.7/bin
./spark-shell
```

If Spark is correctly installed, we should see the following output in the console.

```
....
15/01/17 23:17:46 INFO HttpServer: Starting HTTP Server
15/01/17 23:17:46 INFO Utils: Successfully started ser
vice 'HTTP class server' on port 58132.
Welcome to

      ____              __
     / __/__  ___ _____/ /__
    _\ \/ _ \/ _ `/ __/  '_/
   /___/ .__/\_,_/_/ /_/\_\   version 2.1.0
      /_/

Using Scala version 2.10.4 (Java HotSpot(TM) 64-Bit
Server VM, Java 1.7.0_71)
Type in expressions to have them evaluated.
Type :help for more information.
....
15/01/17 23:17:53 INFO BlockManagerMaster: Registered
BlockManager
15/01/17 23:17:53 INFO SparkILoop: Created spark con
text..
Spark context available as sc.
```

We can type the following commands to check if the Spark shell is working correctly.

```
sc.version
```

Or:

```
sc.appName
```

After this step, we can exit the Spark shell window by typing the following command.

```
:quit
```

To launch the Spark Python shell, we need Python installed. We can download and install Anaconda, which is a free Python distribution and includes several popular Python packages for science, math, engineering, and data analysis.

Then we can run the following commands:

```
c:
cd c:\dev\spark-2.2.0-bin-hadoop2.7
bin\pyspark
```

To exit from Python's Spark shell window, type the following command.

```
:exit()
```

Word-count application

With Spark up and running, we can run data-analysis queries using the Spark API. These are simple commands to read the data from a text file and process it.

Let's use the Spark API to run the popular word-count example. Open a new Spark Scala shell if it's not already running. Here are the commands for this example.

```
import org.apache.spark.SparkContext
import org.apache.spark.SparkContext._

val txtFile = "README.md"
val txtData = sc.textFile(txtFile)
txtData.cache()
```

We call the cache function to store the RDD created in the above step in the cache so Spark doesn't have to compute it every time we use it for further data queries. Note that cache() is a lazy operation. Spark doesn't immediately store the data in memory when we call cache. It actually takes place when an action is called on an RDD.

We can call the count function to see how many lines are there in the text file.

```
txtData.count()
```

Now, we can run the following commands to perform the word count. The count shows up next to each word in the text file.

```
val wcData = txtData.flatMap(l => l.split(" ")).map(word
=> (word, 1)).reduceByKey(_ + _)

wcData.collect().foreach(println)
```

If you want to look at more code examples that use Spark Core API, check out the online Spark documentation.

Conclusions

In this section, we looked at how the Apache Spark framework helps with big-data processing and analysis with its standard API. We also looked at how Spark compares with traditional MapReduce implementation like Apache Hadoop. Spark is based on the same HDFS file storage system as Hadoop, so you can use Spark and MapReduce together if you already have significant investment and infrastructure setup with Hadoop.

You can also combine the Spark processing with Spark SQL, Spark MLlib (for machine learning), and Spark Streaming, as we'll see later on.

With several integrations and adapters on Spark, you can combine it with other technologies. An example of this is to use Spark, Kafka, and Apache Cassandra together where Kafka can be used for the streaming data coming in, Spark for the computation, and a Cassandra NoSQL database for storing the resulting computation data.

References

- Spark homepage
- Spark examples
- Spark Summit 2017 presentation and videos
- Spark on Databricks
- Databricks Community Edition

PART
TWO

Spark SQL

In the first part of this book, we learned about Apache Spark and how it helps organizations with big-data processing analysis.

Spark SQL, part of that Apache Spark big-data framework, is used for structured data processing and allows us to run SQL-like queries on Spark data. We can perform ETL on the data from different formats like JSON, Parquet, or a database and then run ad-hoc querying.

In Part 2, we'll look at the Spark SQL library and how to use it to execute SQL queries against the data stored in batch files, JSON datasets, or Hive tables.

Prior to Spark version 1.3, the Spark SQL module had alpha status but the team has removed that label from the library in the recent updates. Recent releases offer several new features including:

* DataFrames, a programming abstraction that can act as distributed SQL query engine;
* a data-sources API that makes it easier to compute over structured data stored in a wide variety of formats, including Parquet, JSON, and the Apache Avro library; and
* a built-in JDBC server that makes it easy to connect to the structured data stored in relational-database tables and analyze big data with the traditional BI tools.

The two main components when using Spark SQL are DataFrame and SQLContext.

DataFrame

A DataFrame is a distributed collection of data organized into named columns. It is based on the data-frame concept in R language and is similar to a database table in a relational database.

SchemaRDD, found in prior versions of Spark SQL API, has been re-named DataFrame.

DataFrames can be converted to RDDs by calling the RDD method, which returns the content of the DataFrame as an RDD of rows.

DataFrames can be created from different data sources such as:

* existing RDDs,

- structured data files,
- JSON datasets,
- Hive tables, and
- external databases

The Spark SQL and DataFrame APIs are available in Scala, Java, Python, and R.

In addition to DataFrame, Spark also provides the Dataset API. A Dataset is a distributed collection of data similar to RDDs but which uses an encoder to serialize the objects. The Dataset API is available in Scala and Java. Spark SQL supports methods for converting existing RDDs into Datasets.

The Spark SQL code examples we discuss in this section use the Spark Scala shell program.

SQLContext

Spark SQL provides SQLContext to encapsulate all relational functionality in Spark. You create the SQLContext from the existing SparkContext that we have seen in the previous examples. The following code snippet shows how to create a SQLContext object.

```
val sqlContext = new org.apache.spark.sql.SQLContext(sc)
```

There is also HiveContext, which provides a superset of the functionality provided by SQLContext. It can be used to write queries using the HiveQL parser and to read data from Hive tables.

Note that we don't need an existing Hive environment to use HiveContext in Spark programs.

JDBC data source

The Spark SQL library also includes data sources such as the JDBC data source.

We can use the JDBC data source to read data from relational databases using the JDBC API. This approach is preferred over using JdbcRDD because the data source returns the results as a DataFrame that can be processed in Spark SQL or joined with other data sources.

Sample Spark SQL application

In the previous section, we installed the Spark framework on a local machine. For the code examples in this section, we will use the same Spark shell to execute the Spark SQL programs.

To make sure Spark shell program has enough memory, use the driver-memory command-line argument when running `spark-shell`, as shown in the following commands.

For Windows:

```
spark-shell.cmd --driver-memory 1G
```

For Linux/macOS:

```
./spark-shell --driver-memory 1G
```

Spark SQL application

Once the Spark shell launches, we can run the data-analysis queries using the Spark SQL API.

For the first example, we'll load customer data from a text file and create a DataFrame object from the dataset. Then we can run DataFrame functions as specific queries to select the data.

Let's look at the contents of a sample text file called customers.txt.

```
100, John Smith, Austin, TX, 78727
200, Joe Johnson, Dallas, TX, 75201
300, Bob Jones, Houston, TX, 77028
400, Andy Davis, San Antonio, TX, 78227
500, James Williams, Austin, TX, 78727
```

The following code shows the Spark SQL commands we can run on the Spark shell console.

```scala
// Create the SQLContext first from the existing Spark
Context
val sqlContext = new org.apache.spark.sql.SQLContext(sc)

// Import statement to implicitly convert an RDD to a
DataFrame
import sqlContext.implicits._

// Create a custom class to represent the Customer
case class Customer(customer_id: Int, name: String,
city: String, state: String, zip_code: String)

// Create a DataFrame of Customer objects from the data
set text file.
val dfCustomers = sc.textFile("data/customers.txt").
map(_.split(",")).map(p => Customer(p(0).trim.toInt,
p(1), p(2), p(3), p(4))).toDF()

// Register DataFrame as a table.
dfCustomers.registerTempTable("customers")

// Display the content of DataFrame
dfCustomers.show()

// Print the DF schema
dfCustomers.printSchema()

// Select customer name column
dfCustomers.select("name").show()

// Select customer name and city columns
dfCustomers.select("name", "city").show()

// Select a customer by id
dfCustomers.filter(dfCustomers("customer_id").equal
To(500)).show()

// Count the customers by zip code
dfCustomers.groupBy("zip_code").count().show()
```

In the above example, the schema is inferred using the reflection. We can also programmatically specify the schema of the dataset. This is useful when the custom classes cannot be defined ahead of time because the structure of data is encoded in a string.

Following code example shows how to specify the schema using the new data type classes StructType, StringType, and StructField.

```
//
// Programmatically Specifying the Schema
//

// Create SQLContext from the existing SparkContext.
val sqlContext = new org.apache.spark.sql.SQLContext(sc)

// Create an RDD
val rddCustomers = sc.textFile("data/customers.txt")

// The schema is encoded in a string
val schemaString = "customer_id name city state zip_
code"

// Import Spark SQL data types and Row.
import org.apache.spark.sql._

import org.apache.spark.sql.types._;

// Generate the schema based on the string of schema
val schema = StructType(schemaString.split(" ").map(
fieldName => StructField(fieldName, StringType, true)))

// Convert records of the RDD (rddCustomers) to Rows.
val rowRDD = rddCustomers.map(_.split(",")).map(p =>
Row(p(0).trim,p(1),p(2),p(3),p(4)))

// Apply the schema to the RDD.
val dfCustomers = sqlContext.createDataFrame(rowRDD,
schema)

// Register the DataFrames as a table.
dfCustomers.registerTempTable("customers")

// SQL statements can be run by using the sql methods
```

```
provided by sqlContext.
val custNames = sqlContext.sql("SELECT name FROM
customers")

// The results of SQL queries are DataFrames and support
all the normal RDD operations.
// The columns of a row in the result can be accessed by
ordinal.
custNames.map(t => "Name: " + t(0)).collect().
foreach(println)

// SQL statements can be run by using the sql methods
provided by sqlContext.
val customersByCity = sqlContext.sql("SELECT name,zip_
code FROM customers ORDER BY zip_code")

// The results of SQL queries are DataFrames and support
all the normal RDD operations.
// The columns of a row in the result can be accessed by
ordinal.
customersByCity.map(t => t(0) + "," + t(1)).collect().
foreach(println)
```

We can also load the data from other data sources like JSON data files, Hive tables, or even relational database tables using the JDBC data source.

Spark SQL provides a nice SQL interface for interacting with data that's loaded from diverse data sources, using the familiar SQL query syntax. This is especially useful for non-technical project members like data analysts as well as DBAs.

Conclusions

The Spark SQL library in the Apache Spark framework provides an SQL interface to interact with big data using the familiar SQL query syntax. Spark SQL is a powerful library that non-technical team members like business and data analysts can use to analyze large datasets.

References

- Spark SQL homepage
- Spark SQL, DataFrames, and Datasets Guide
- "Big Data Processing with Apache Spark — Part 1: Introduction"

PART
THREE

Spark Streaming

The Apache Spark framework (Part 1) and the SQL interface to access data using Spark SQL library (Part 2) are based on processing static data in a batch mode, for example as an hourly or a daily job. But what about real-time data streams that need to be processed on the fly to perform analysis and reveal evidence for data-driven business decisions?

With streaming-data processing, computing is done in real time as data arrives rather than as an offline batch process. Real-time data processing and analysis is becoming a critical component of the big-data strategy for many organizations.

This section will cover the real-time data analytics using one of the libraries from Apache Spark, called Spark Streaming.

We'll look at webserver log analysis use case to show how Spark Streaming can help with analyzing data streams that are generated in a continuous manner.

Streaming-data analysis

Streaming data is basically a continuous group of data records generated from sources like sensors, server traffic, and online searches. Examples of streaming data are user activity on websites, monitoring data, server logs, and other event data.

Streaming-data processing applications help with live dashboards, real-time online recommendations, and instant fraud detection.

If we are building applications to collect, process, and analyze streaming data in real time, we need to take into account design considerations that are different than those for applications used to process static batch data.

Streaming-data processing frameworks include Apache Samza, Apache Storm, and Spark Streaming.

Spark Streaming

Spark Streaming is an extension of the core Spark API. Spark Streaming makes it easy to build fault-tolerant processing of real-time data streams.

Figure 3.1 shows how Spark Streaming fits into the Apache Spark ecosystem.

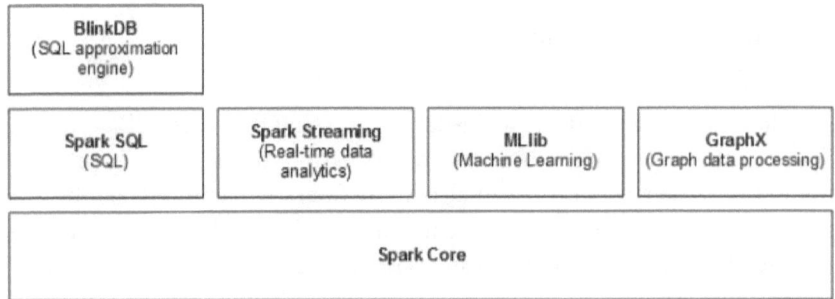

Figure 3.1. The Spark ecosystem with the Spark Streaming library.

As of version 2.0, Spark supports a new streaming library called Structured Streaming, which offers a scalable and fault-tolerant stream-processing engine based on Spark SQL. We can use the Dataset and DataFrame APIs in Scala, Java, Python, or R languages to write the streaming aggregations. Structured Streaming provides exactly-once stream processing without the user having to reason about streaming.

Spark Streaming works by dividing the live stream of data into batches (called micro-batches) of a pre-defined interval (N seconds) and then treating each batch of data as a RDD. We can process these RDDs using operations like map, reduce, reduceByKey, join, and window. The results of these RDD operations are returned in batches. We usually store these results in a data store for further analysis, to generate reports and dashboards, or to send event-based alerts.

It's important to decide the time interval for Spark Streaming, based on use case and data-processing requirements. If the value of N is too low, then the micro-batches will not have enough data to give meaningful results during the analysis.

Other stream-processing frameworks process the data streams per event rather than as a micro-batch. With Spark Streaming's micro-batch approach, we can use other Spark libraries (like the core, machine-learning, etc. libraries) with the Spark Streaming API in the same application.

Streaming data can come from many different sources, including:

- Kafka,
- Flume,
- Twitter,
- ZeroMQ,
- Amazon's Kinesis, and
- TCP sockets.

Another advantage of using a big-data processing framework like Apache Spark is that we can combine batch processing and streaming processing in the same system. We can also apply Spark's machine-learning and graph-processing algorithms on data streams. We'll discuss those libraries, called MLlib and GraphX respectively, in later sections of this book.

The Spark Streaming architecture is shown in Figure 3.2.

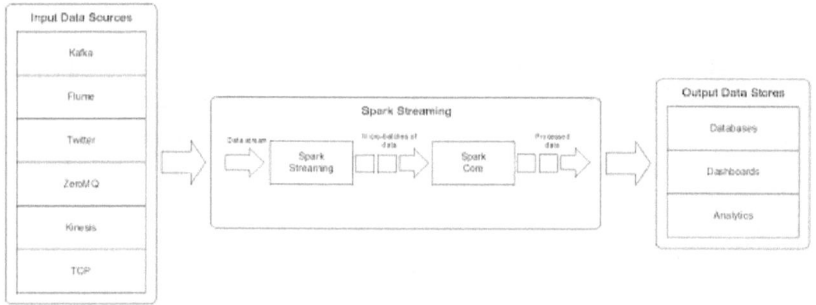

Figure 3.2. How Spark Streaming works.

Spark Streaming use cases

Spark Streaming is becoming the platform of choice for data processing and analysis of real-time data received from Internet of Things (IoT) and sensors. It is used in a variety of use cases and business applications.

Some of the most interesting use cases of Spark Streaming include the following:

- Uber, the ride-sharing service, uses Spark Streaming in their continuous-streaming ETL pipeline to collect terabytes of event data every day from their mobile users for real-time telemetry analysis.

- Pinterest uses Spark Streaming, MemSQL, and Apache Kafka technologies to provide real-time insight into how their users are engaging with pins across the globe.

- Netflix uses Kafka and Spark Streaming to build a real-time online movie recommendation and data-monitoring solution that processes billions of events received per day from different data sources.

Other examples of Spark Streaming in use include:

- supply-chain analysis,
- real-time security-intelligence operations to find threats,
- ad-auction platforms, and
- real-time video analysis to help provide personalized, interactive experiences to the viewers.

Let's take a look at Spark Streaming architecture and API methods. To write Spark Streaming programs, there are two components we need to know about: DStream and StreamingContext.

DStream

DStream (short for "discretized stream") is the basic abstraction in Spark Streaming and represents a continuous stream of data. DStreams can be created either from input data streams from sources such as Kafka, Flume, and Kinesis, or by applying operations on other DStreams. Internally, a DStream is represented as a sequence of RDD objects.

Similar to the transformation and action operations on RDDs, DStreams support the following operations:

- `map`,
- `flatMap`,
- `filter`,
- `count`,
- `reduce`,
- `countByValue`,
- `reduceByKey`,

- `join`, and
- `updateStateByKey`.

StreamingContext

Similar to SparkContext for regular Spark programs, StreamingContext is the main entry point for all streaming functionality.

StreamingContext has built-in methods for receiving streaming data in a Spark Streaming program.

Using this context, we can create a DStream that represents streaming data from a TCP source, specified by hostname and port number. For example, if we were using a tool like Ncat to test the Spark Streaming program, we would receive a data stream from the machine where Ncat is running (for example, localhost) and port number of 9999.

When the code is executed, Spark Streaming only sets up the computation it will perform when it is started, and no real processing is done yet. To start the processing after all the transformations have been set up, we finally call the `start()` method to start the computation and the `awaitTermination()` method to wait for the computation to terminate.

Spark Streaming API

Spark Streaming comes with several API methods that are useful for processing data streams. There are RDD-like operations like `map`, `flatMap`, `filter`, `count`, `reduce`, `groupByKey`, `reduceByKey`, `sortByKey`, and `join`. It also provides additional APIs to process the streaming data based on window and stateful operations. These include `window`, `countByWindow`, `reduceByWindow`, `countByValueAndWindow`, `reduceByKeyAndWindow`, and `updateStateByKey`.

The Spark Streaming library is currently supported in Scala, Java, and Python. Here are the links to Spark Streaming API in each of these languages:

- Spark Streaming Scala API
- Java API
- Python API

Steps in a Spark Streaming program

Before we discuss the sample application, let's take a look at the steps involved in a typical Spark Streaming program.

1. We use StreamingContext to process the real-time data streams. So, the first step is to initialize the StreamingContext object using two parameters: SparkContext and sliding-interval time. Sliding interval sets the update window in which we process the data coming in as streams. Once the context is initialized, no new computations can be defined or added to the existing context. Also, only one Streaming-Context object can be active at any time.

2. After we define the Spark Streaming context, we specify the input data sources by creating input DStreams. In our sample application, the input data source is a log-message generator that uses the Apache Kafka distributed database and messaging system. The log-generator program creates random log messages to simulate a webserver run-time environment that continuously generates log messages as various web applications serve the user traffic.

3. Define the computations to be performed on the input DStream using Spark Streaming transformations API like `map` and `reduce`.

4. After defining the streaming computation logic, we can start receiving the data and process it using `start` method in the Streaming-Context object created in step 1.

5. Finally, we wait for the streaming-data processing to be stopped using the `awaitTermination` method of the StreamingContext object.

Sample application

The sample application we will consider is a server-log processing and analysis program. We can use it for real-time monitoring of application server logs and to analyze data in those logs. These log messages are considered time-series data, which is defined as a sequence of successive measurements captured over a specified time interval.

Time-series data examples include sensor data, weather information, and click-stream data. Time-series analysis is about processing the time-series data to extract insights that can be used for business decisions. This data can also be used to predict future values based on historical data.

With streaming-data processing, we don't need hourly or daily batch jobs to process the server logs. Spark Streaming receives continuously generated data, processes it, and computes log statistics to provide insight into the data.

To follow a standard example of analyzing server logs, we'll use the log-analysis application mentioned on the Databricks Reference Apps website as a reference for our sample application. This application already has the code to parse log messages, which we'll reuse in our application. The reference application is an excellent resource for learning more about the Spark framework in general and Spark Streaming in particular. For more details on Databricks Spark reference applications, check out the website.

Use case

The use case for the sample application is a log-analysis and statistics generator. In the sample application, we analyze the webserver logs to compute the following statistics for further data analysis and create reports and dashboards:

- response counts by different HTTP response codes,
- response content size,
- IP addresses of clients to assess where the most web traffic is coming from, and
- top endpoint URLs to identify which services are accessed more than others.

Unlike in the previous two sections in this book, we will use Java instead of Scala for creating the Spark program in this section. We'll also run the program as a stand-alone application instead of running the code from the console window. This is how we would deploy Spark programs in test and production environments. A shell-console interface (using Scala, Python, or R languages) is for local developer testing only.

ZooKeeper and Kafka technologies

We will use ZooKeeper and Apache Kafka in our sample application to demonstrate how the Spark Streaming library is used for processing real-time data streams.

ZooKeeper is a centralized service that provides reliable distributed coordination for distributed applications.

Apache Kafka, the messaging system we use in the sample application, depends on ZooKeeper for configuration details across the cluster. Kafka is a real-time, fault-tolerant, scalable messaging system for moving data in real time. It's a good candidate for use cases like capturing user activity on websites, logs, stock-ticker data, and instrumentation data.

Kafka works like a distributed database and is based on a partitioned and replicated low-latency commit log. When we post a message to Kafka, it's replicated to different servers in the cluster and at the same time it's also committed to disk.

Kakfa provides a client API as well as a data-transfer framework called Kafka Connect.

The Kafka framework includes Java clients (for both message producers and consumers) and non-Java clients are available as independent open-source projects. We will use the Java producer client API in our sample application.

Kafka Connect is a framework for streaming data between Kafka and external data systems to support the data pipelines in organizations. It includes import and export connectors to move datasets into and out of Kafka. Kafka Connect can run as a stand-alone process or as a distributed service and supports a REST interface to submit the connectors to a Kafka Connect cluster using a REST API.

Spark Streaming

We'll use the Spark Streaming Java API to receive the data streams, calculate the log statistics, and run queries to discover, for example, from which IP addresses most web requests are coming.

Table 3.1 shows the technologies and tools and their versions used in the sample applications.

Technology	Version	URL
ZooKeeper	3.4.6	https://zookeeper.apache.org/doc/r3.4.6/
Kafka	2.10	http://kafka.apache.org/downloads.html
Spark Streaming	2.2	http://spark.apache.org/docs/latest/streaming-programming-guide.html
JDK	8	http://www.oracle.com/technetwork/java/javase/downloads/index.html
Maven	3.3.3	http://archive.apache.org/dist/maven/maven-3/3.3.3/

Table 3.1. Spark Streaming sample application technologies and tools.

Figure 3.3 shows the different architecture components of our Spark Streaming sample application.

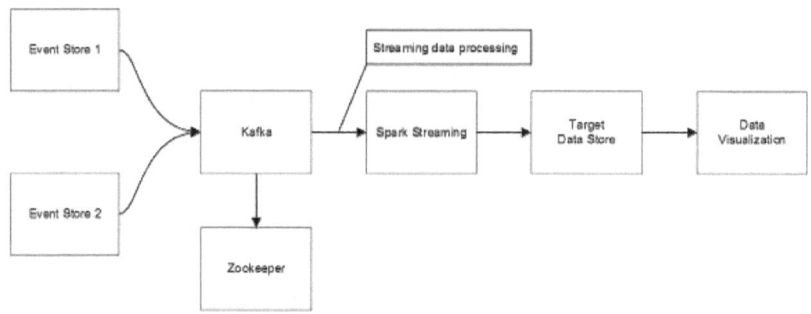

Figure 3.3. Spark Streaming sample application architecture.

Spark Streaming application runtime

To set up the Java project locally, download the code for the Databricks reference application from GitHub. Once we get that code, we'll need two additional Java classes to run our sample application: the log generator (`SparkStreamingKafkaLogGenerator.java`) and log analyzer (`SparkStreamingKafkaLogAnalyzer.java`).

These files are provided as a zip file (spark-streaming-kafka-sample-app. zip) on this book's website. To run the sample application on a local machine, use the link to download the zip file, extract the Java classes, and add them to the Java project created in the previous step.

The sample application can be executed on different operating systems. I ran the application in both Windows and Linux (CentOS VM) environments.

The code examples discussed in this section are available at the following Github project:

https://github.com/spenchikala/big-data-processing-spark-mini-book

ZooKeeper commands

I used ZooKeeper version 3.4.6 in the sample application. To start the server, set two environment variables, `JAVA_HOME` and `ZOOKEEPER_HOME`, to point to the respective JDK and ZooKeeper installation directories. Then navigate to the ZooKeeper home directory and run the following command to start the ZooKeeper server.

```
bin\zkServer.cmd
```

If you are using a Linux or macOS environment, the command is:

```
bin/zkServer.sh start
```

Kafka server commands

I used Kafka version 2.10-0.9.0.0, which is based on Scala 2.10. The Scala version used with Kafka is important because we get run-time errors when executing the Spark Streaming program if the correct version is not used. Here are the steps to start the Kafka server instance:

Open a new command prompt.

Set `JAVA_HOME` and `KAFKA_HOME` variables.

Navigate to the Kafka home directory.

Run the following command.

```
bin\windows\kafka-server-start.bat config\
server.properties
```

For a Linux/macOS environment, the command is:

```
bin/kafka-server-start.sh config/server.properties
```

Log-generator commands

The next step in our sample application is to run the message-log generator.

The log generator creates test log messages with different HTTP response codes (like 200, 401, and 404) with different endpoint URLs.

Before we run the log generator, we need to create a new Kafka Topic to which we can post the messages.

Similar to the previous sequence of steps, open a new command prompt, set JAVA_HOME and KAFKA_HOME variables, and navigate to the Kafka home directory. Then run the following command to view the topics available in the Kafka server.

```
bin\windows\kafka-run-class.bat kafka.admin.TopicCommand
--zookeeper localhost:2181 -list
```

In Linux/macOS, it's:

```
bin/kafka-run-class.sh kafka.admin.TopicCommand --zoo
keeper localhost:2181 -list
```

We will create a new topic called spark-streaming-sample-topic using the following command.

```
bin\windows\kafka-run-class.bat kafka.admin.TopicCommand
--zookeeper localhost:2181 --replication-factor 1 --par
titions 1 --create --topic spark-streaming-sample-topic
```

Or in Linux/macOS:

```
bin/kafka-run-class.sh kafka.admin.TopicCommand --zoo
keeper localhost:2181 --replication-factor 1 --parti
tions 1 --create --topic spark-streaming-sample-topic
```

You can run the "list topics" command again to see if the new topic has been correctly created.

Once the topic has been created, we can run the log-generator program. We do this by executing the Java class called `SparkStreamingKafka-LogGenerator`. The log-generator class takes the following four arguments to specify the configuration parameters:

- Group ID: `spark-streaming-sample-group`
- Topic: `spark-streaming-sample-topic`
- Number of iterations: 50
- Interval: 1000

Open a new command prompt to run the log generator. We will set three environment variables (`JAVA_HOME, MAVEN_HOME`, and `KAFKA_HOME`) for JDK, Maven, and Kakfa directories respectively. Then navigate to sample project root directory (for example, `c:\dev\projects\spark-streaming-kafka-sample-app`) and run the following command.

```
mvn exec:java -Dexec.mainClass=com.sparkstreaming.
kafka.example.SparkStreamingKafkaLogGenerator -Dexec.
args="spark-streaming-sample-groupid spark-stream
ing-sample-topic 50 1000"
```

Once the log-generator program is running, we should see the sample log messages with the debug messages shown on the console. This is only sample code, so the log messages are randomly generated to simulate the continuous flow of data from an event store like a webserver.

Figure 3.4 is a screenshot of a log-message producer generating log messages.

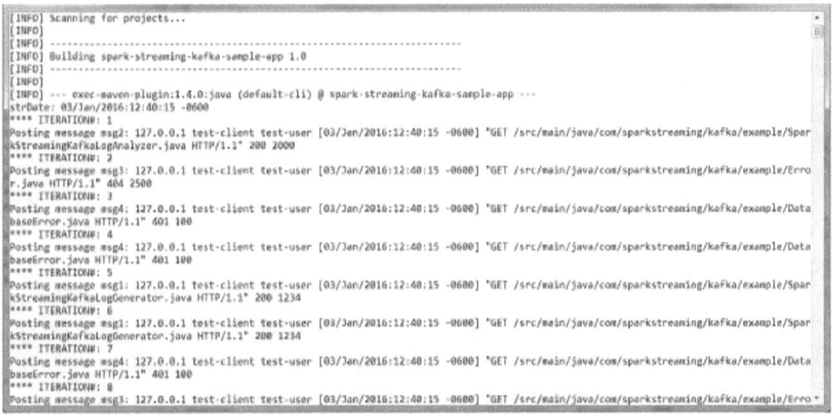

Figure 3.4. Output of a Spark Streaming log generator.

Spark Streaming commands

This consumer of log messages uses the Spark Streaming API. We use a Java class called SparkStreamingKafkaLogAnalyzer to receive the data streams from the Kafka server and process them to create log statistics.

Sparking Streaming program processes the server log messages and generates cumulative log statistics like size of web-request content (minimum, maximum, and average), counts of response code, IP addresses, and top endpoints.

We create the Spark context using local[*] parameter, which detects the number of cores in the local system and uses them to run the program.

To run the Spark Streaming Java class, we will need the following JAR files in the classpath:

- kafka_2.10-0.9.0.0.jar,
- kafka-clients-0.9.0.0.jar,
- metrics-core-2.2.0.jar,
- spark-streaming-kafka_2.10-1.4.0.jar, and
- zkclient-0.3.jar.

I ran the program from Eclipse IDE after adding the above JAR files to the classpath. Log analysis of the Spark Streaming program is shown in Figure 3.5.

Figure 3.5. Spark Streaming log-analysis output.

Visualization of Spark Streaming applications

When the Spark Streaming program is running, we can check the Spark console to view the details of the Spark jobs.

Open a new web browser window and navigate to URL http://localhost:4040 to access the Spark console website.

Let's look at some of the graphs of the Spark Streaming program statistics.

The first visualization is the DAG (direct acyclic graph) of a specific job that shows the dependency graph of different operations we ran in the program, like `map`, `window`, and `foreachRDD`. Figure 3.6 shows the screenshot of this.

Figure 3.6. DAG visualization graph of the Spark Streaming job.

The next chart records streaming statistics and includes the input rate as number of events per second, with processing time in milliseconds.

Figure 3.7 shows these statistics during the execution of our Spark Streaming program when the streaming data is not being generated (left) and when the data stream is being sent to Kafka and processed by the Spark Streaming consumer (right).

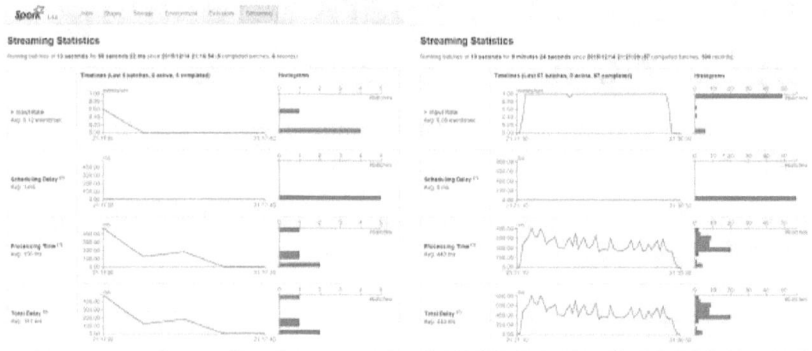

Figure 3.7. A Spark Streaming visualization showing streaming statistics for the sample program.

Conclusions

The Spark Streaming library, part of the Apache Spark ecosystem, is used to process real-time streaming data. In this section, we learned about how to use the Spark Streaming API to process data generated by server logs and perform analytics on the real-time data streams.

References

- "Big Data Processing with Apache Spark — Part 1: Introduction"
- "Big Data Processing with Apache Spark — Part 2: Spark SQL"
- Apache Spark homepage
- Spark Streaming homepage
- Spark Streaming Programming Guide
- Spark Streaming Scala code examples
- Spark Streaming Java code examples
- Databricks Reference Apps
- Tagging and Processing Data in Real-Time Using Spark Streaming (Spark Summit 2015 presentation)
- A Quick Guide to Spark Streaming (MapR)

PART
FOUR

Spark Machine Learning

Machine learning, predictive analytics, and data science have been gaining attention in recent years for solving real-world problems in different business domains. Spark MLlib, Spark's machine-learning library, includes several different machine-learning algorithms for collaborative filtering, clustering, classification, and other tasks.

In previous sections, we've looked at what the Apache Spark framework is (Part 1), how to leverage the SQL interface to access data using the Spark SQL library (Part 2), and real-time data processing and analysis of streaming data using Spark Streaming (Part 3).

In this section, we'll discuss machine learning and how to use the Apache Spark MLlib library for predictive analysis. We will use a sample application to illustrate the powerful API that Spark provides for machine learning.

The Spark machine-learning API includes two packages: `spark.mllib` and `spark.ml`.

The `spark.mllib` package contains the original Spark machine-learning API built on RDDs. It offers machine-learning techniques, which include correlation, classification and regression, collaborative filtering, clustering, and dimensionality reduction.

On the other hand, the `spark.ml` package provides a machine-learning API built on DataFrames, which are becoming the core of the Spark SQL library. This package can be used to develop and manage machine-learning pipelines. It also provides feature extractors, transformers, selectors, and machine-learning techniques like classification, regression, and clustering.

We'll focus on Spark MLlib in this section and discuss the various machine-learning techniques this package brings to the table. In the next section, we'll cover the `spark.ml` package and look at how to create and manage data pipelines.

Machine learning and data science

Machine learning is about learning from existing data to make predictions. It's based on creating models from input datasets for data-driven decision making.

Data science is the discipline of extracting the knowledge from large datasets (structured or unstructured) to provide insights to business teams and influence business strategies and roadmaps. The role of data scientist is more critical than ever in solving problems that are not easy to solve using traditional numerical methods.

There are different types of machine-learning models:

- supervised learning,
- unsupervised learning,
- semi-supervised learning, and
- reinforcement learning.

Supervised learning is used to predict an outcome by training the program using a pre-existing training set of labeled data. We then use the program to predict the label for a new, unlabeled dataset. There are two sub-models of supervised machine learning: regression and classification.

Unsupervised learning is used to find hidden patterns and correlations within the raw data. No training data used in this model, so this technique is based on unlabeled data. Algorithms like k-means and principle component analysis (PCA) fall into this category.

Semi-supervised learning uses both supervised and unsupervised learning models for predictive analysis. It uses labeled and unlabeled datasets for training, typically using a small amount of labeled data with a large amount of unlabeled data. It can be used for machine-learning methods like classification and regression.

Reinforcement learning is used to learn how to maximize a numerical reward by trying different actions and discovering which actions result in the maximum reward.

The following table shows examples of problems these machine-learning models can be used to solve.

ML Model	Examples
Supervised learning	Fraud detection
Unsupervised learning	Social-network applications, language prediction
Semi-supervised learning	Image categorization, voice recognition
Reinforcement learning	Artificial intelligence

Table 4.1. Applications of machine-learning models.

Machine-learning algorithms

Several algorithms help with machine learning.

Naive Bayes is a supervised-learning algorithm used for classification. It's based on applying Bayes's theorem and a set of conditional independence assumptions.

The k-means algorithm or k-means clustering creates k groups from a set of objects so that the members of each group are more similar to each other.

A support-vector machine (SVM) is a supervised-learning algorithm used to find the boundary that separates classes by as wide a margin as possible. Given a set of training examples, each marked as belonging to one of two categories, an SVM training algorithm builds a model that assigns new examples into one category or the other. Applications of SVM include bioinformatics, text analysis, and image recognition.

Decision trees are used in many types of machine-learning problems, including multiclass classification. Spark MLlib supports both a basic decision-tree algorithm and ensembles of trees. Two ensemble algorithms are available: gradient-boosted trees and random forests.

As documented at Machine Learning Mastery, here is a summary of all the machine-learning styles, problems, and solution methods.

ML Model	Problems	Algorithms
Supervised learning	Classification, regression, anomaly detection	Logistic regression, back-propagation neural network
Unsupervised learning	Clustering, dimensionality reduction	k-means, Apriori algorithm
Semi-supervised learning	Classification, regression	Self-training, semi-supervised support-vector machines (S3VMs)

Table 4.2. Machine-learning styles, problems, and methods.

Steps in a machine-learning program

When working on machine-learning projects, other tasks like data preparation, cleansing, and analysis are also important tasks beyond the actual learning models and algorithms used to solve the business problems.

The following are the steps performed in a typical machine-learning program:

1. featurization,
2. training, and
3. model evaluation.

Figure 4.1 shows the process flow of a typical machine-learning solution.

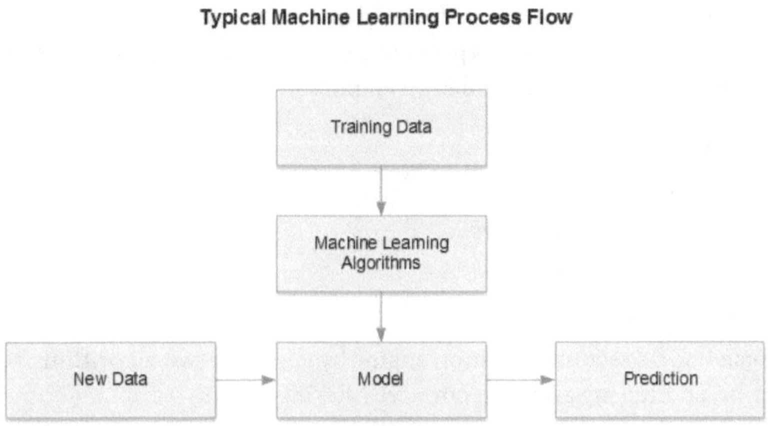

Typical Machine Learning Process Flow

Figure 4.1. Machine-learning process flow.

It's important to know that if the raw data isn't cleaned or prepared before running a machine-learning algorithm, the resulting pattern will not be accurate or useful, and it may miss some anomalies.

The quality of training data we provide to machine-learning programs also plays a critical role in the prediction results. If the training data is not random enough, the resulting patterns won't be accurate. And if the dataset is too small, the machine-learning program may give inaccurate predictions.

Use cases

The business use cases for machine learning span different domains and scenarios including recommendation engines (such as this food recommendation engine), predictive analysis (for example, predicting stock prices or flight delays), targeted advertising, fraud detection, image and video recognition, self-driving cars, and other forms of artificial intelligence.

Let's look at two popular applications, a recommendation engine and fraud detection, in more detail.

Recommendation engines

Recommendation engines use the attributes of an item or a user or the behavior of a user or the user's peers to make predictions. Different factors drive an effective recommendation engine. Some of these factors include:

- peer analysis,
- customer behavior,
- corporate deals or offers,
- item clustering, and
- market/store factors.

We can build a recommendation engine by engaging two algorithms: content-based filtering and collaborative filtering.

Content-based filtering is based on how similar the usage and ratings of a particular item are to other items. The model uses the content attributes of items (such as categories, tags, descriptions, and other data) to generate a matrix that relates each item to other items and calculates similarity based on the ratings provided. Then the most similar items are listed together with a similarity score. Items with the highest score are most similar.

Movie recommendation is a good example of this model. It can advise that users who liked a particular movie liked these other movies as well.

Content-based filtering doesn't take into account the overall behavior of other users, so its models don't provide personalized recommendations like collaborative filtering and other models do.

On the other hand, collaborative-filtering models do predict and recommend specific items or users based on similarity to other items or users. The filter applies weights based on the "peer user" preferences. The assumption is that users with similar profiles or behaviors will also have similar item preferences.

An example of this model is the recommendations on e-commerce websites like Amazon. When we search for an item on the website, we see a listing called "Customers who viewed this item also bought".

Items with the highest recommendation score are the most relevant to the user in context.

Collaborative-filtering solutions perform better than other models. Spark MLlib implements a collaborative-filtering algorithm called alternating least squares (ALS). There are two variations of the entries in collaborative filtering, called explicit and implicit feedback. Explicit feedback is based on the direct preferences given by the user to the item (like a movie). Explicit feedback is nice, but many times it's skewed because users who strongly like or dislike a product tend to review it most often. We don't get the opinion of the many people in the center of the bell curve of preference data points.

Implicit feedback includes a user's views, clicks, likes, etc. Implicit feedback often is used for predictive analysis because of how easy it is to gather this type of data.

There are also model-based methods for recommendation engines. These often incorporate methods from collaborative and content-based filtering. A model-based approach gets the best of both worlds: the power and performance of collaborative filtering and the flexibility and adaptability of content-based filtering. Deep-learning techniques are good examples of this model.

You can also integrate other algorithms like k-means clustering into the recommendation engine to further refine predictions. The k-means algorithm works by partitioning N observations into k clusters in which each observation belongs to the cluster with the nearest mean. Using the k-means technique, we can find similar items or users based on their attributes.

Figure 4.2 shows the different components of a recommendation engine: user factors, other factors like market data, and algorithms.

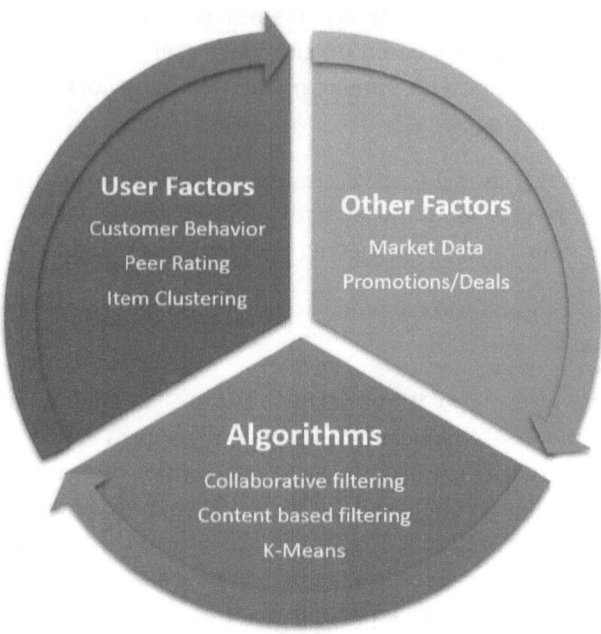

Figure 4.2. Components of a recommendation engine.

Fraud detection

Fraud detection is another important use case of machine learning. It addresses a critical problem in the financial industry quickly and accurately. Financial-services organizations only have few hundred milliseconds to determine if a particular online transaction is legitimate or a fraud.

Neural-network techniques are used for point-of-sale (POS) fraud detection. Organizations like PayPal use different types of machine-learning algorithms for risk management, like linear, neural network, and deep learning.

The Spark MLlib library provides several algorithms for solving this use case, including linear SVMs, logistic regression, decision trees, and naive Bayes. Ensemble models (which combine the predictions of a set of models) such as random forests or gradient-boosting trees are also available.

As recommended in this article, we can follow the steps listed below to implement machine-learning solutions in our own projects.

1. Select the programming language.
2. Select the appropriate algorithm or algorithms.
3. Select the problem.
4. Research the algorithms.
5. Unit-test all the functions in the machine-learning solution.

Let's look at how the Apache Spark framework implements the machine-learning algorithms.

Spark MLlib

MLlib is Spark's machine-learning library. Its goal is to make practical machine learning scalable and easy. It consists of common learning algorithms and utilities, including classification, regression, clustering, collaborative filtering, dimensionality reduction, and lower-level optimization primitives and higher-level pipeline APIs.

Like we learned earlier, there are two ways to use Spark's machine-learning API: Spark MLlib and `spark.ml`.

In addition to various algorithms, Spark MLlib supports data-processing functions and data analysis utilities and tools:

- frequent item-set mining via FP-growth and association rules,
- sequential pattern mining via PrefixSpan,
- summary statistics and hypothesis testing,
- feature transformations, and
- model evaluation and hyper-parameter tuning.

Figure 4.3 shows the Apache Spark framework with the Spark MLlib library.

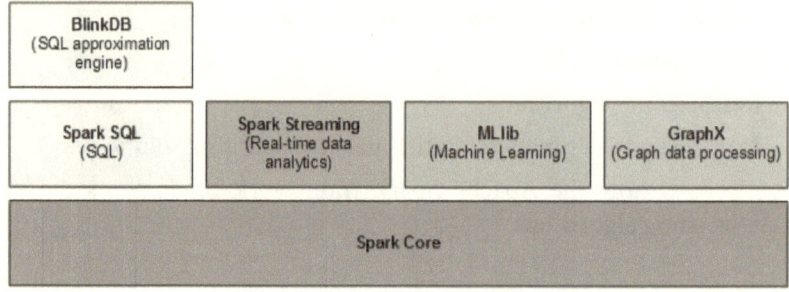

Figure 4.3. The Spark ecosystem with the Spark machine-learning library.

The Spark MLlib API is available in the Scala, Java, and Python programming languages. Here are the links to the API in each of these languages:

- Scala API
- Java API
- Python API

Sample application

We'll develop a sample machine-learning application using a classification technique (collaborative filtering) to derive movies to recommend to a user based on other users' movie ratings.

Our recommendation engine will use the ALS (alternating least squares) machine-learning algorithm.

The datasets used in the code example in this section are neither large nor complicated, but Spark MLlib can be used for any complex problems that deal with data in several dimensions and with complex predictor functions. Remember, machine learning can be used to solve problems that cannot be solved by numerical means alone.

To keep the machine-learning application simple so that we can focus on the Spark MLlib API, we'll follow the Movie Recommendations example discussed in a past Spark Summit workshop. This exercise is a good way to learn more about Spark MLlib. For more details on the sample application, visit its GitHub website.

Use case

We want to implement a recommendation engine. Recommendation engines are used to predict unknown user-item associations (for example, movie ratings) based on known user-item associations. They can make predictions based on a user's preference for other items and other users' preferences for this specific item. The engine builds a prediction model based on known data (called "training data") and then makes predictions for unknown user-item associations (called "test data").

Our program includes the following steps to arrive at the top movie recommendations for the user:

1. Load the movies data file.
2. Load the data file with ratings provided by a specific user.
3. Load the ratings data provided by other users (community).
4. Combine the user ratings with community ratings in a single RDD.
5. Train the model with the ALS algorithm acting on the ratings data.
6. Identify the movies not rated by a particular user (`userId=1`)
7. Predict the ratings of the items not rated by user.
8. Get top N recommendations (five, in our example).
9. Display the recommendation data on the console.

If we want to process or further analyze the output data, we can store the results in a NoSQL database like Cassandra or MongoDB.

Datasets

We will use movie datasets provided by MovieLens. There are a few different data files we need for the sample application, available for download from GroupLens Research website. We will use one of the latest datasets (a smaller one with 100k ratings). Download the data zip file from the website.

The following table shows the different datasets used in the application.

#	Dataset	File Name	Description	Data Fields
1	Movies Data	movies.csv	Movie details.	movieId,title,genres
2	User Ratings Data	user-ratings.csv	Ratings by a specific user.	userId,movieId,rating, timestamp
3	Community Ratings Data	ratings.csv	Ratings by other users.	userId,movieId,rating, timestamp

Table 4.3. Datasets used in the sample application.

The user-ratings file is for the user in context. We can update the ratings in this file based on our movie preferences. We'll assign a user ID called "UserId 0" to represent these ratings.

When we run the recommendation program, we'll combine this specific user's ratings data with ratings from the community (other users).

Technologies

We will use Java to write the Spark MLlib program that can be executed as a stand-alone application. The program uses the following MLlib Java classes (all are located in the `org.apache.spark.mllib.recommendation` package):

- `ALS`,
- `MatrixFactorizationModel`, and
- `Rating`.

We will use the following technologies in the sample application to illustrate how to use the Spark MLlib API to perform predictive analysis:

- Apache Spark 2.2,
- Spark Java API,
- JDK 8,
- Apache Maven 3.3.3, and
- Eclipse IDE.

The architecture of the sample application is shown in Figure 4.4.

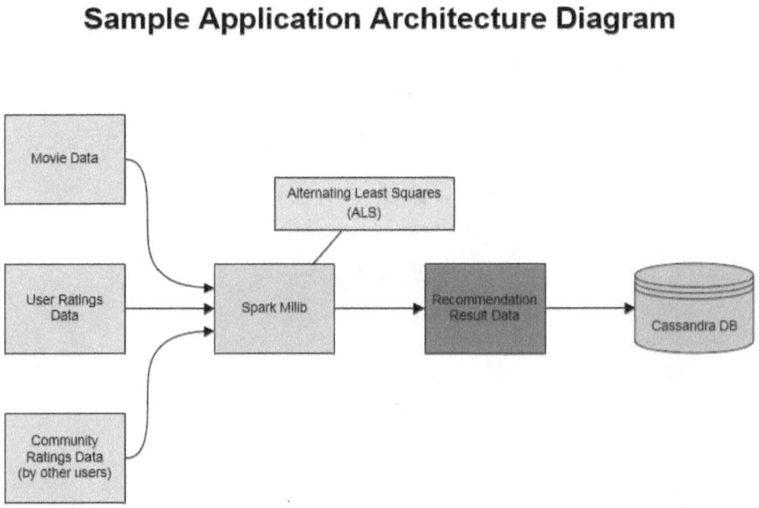

Sample Application Architecture Diagram

Figure 4.4. Architecture of the Spark machine-learning sample application.

There are several implementations of movie-recommendation engines available in the languages supported by Spark: Scala (Databricks and MapR), Java (a set of Spark examples and a Java-based movie recommender), and Python. We'll use one of the Java solutions for our sample application.

Download this Java program from the list of Spark examples. Create a new Maven-based Java project called "spark-mllib-sample-app" and copy the Java class into the project. Modify the Java class to pass in the datasets discussed in the previous section.

The latest version of the code examples discussed in this section are available at the fol-lowing Github project:

https://github.com/spenchikala/big-data-processing-spark-mini-book

Make sure you include the required Spark Java libraries in the dependencies section of Maven pom.xml file. To do a clean build and download Spark library JAR files, you can run the following commands.

Set the environment parameters for JDK (JAVA_HOME), Maven (MAVEN_ HOME), and Spark (SPARK_HOME), which for Windows is:

```
set JAVA_HOME=[JDK_INSTALL_DIRECTORY]
set PATH=%PATH%;%JAVA_HOME%\bin

set MAVEN_HOME=[MAVEN_INSTALL_DIRECTORY]
set PATH=%PATH%;%MAVEN_HOME%\bin

set SPARK_HOME=[SPARK_INSTALL_DIRECTORY]
set PATH=%PATH%;%SPARK_HOME%\bin

cd c:\dev\projects\spark-mllib-sample-app

mvn clean install
mvn eclipse:clean eclipse:eclipse
```

If you are using a Linux or macOS system, you can run:

```
export JAVA_HOME=[JDK_INSTALL_DIRECTORY]
export PATH=$PATH:$JAVA_HOME/bin

export MAVEN_HOME=[MAVEN_INSTALL_DIRECTORY]
export PATH=$PATH:$MAVEN_HOME/bin

export SPARK_HOME=[SPARK_INSTALL_DIRECTORY]
export PATH=$PATH:$SPARK_HOME/bin

cd /Users/USER_NAME/spark-mllib-sample-app

mvn clean install
mvn eclipse:clean eclipse:eclipse
```

If application build is successful, the packaged JAR file will be created in the **target** directory.

We will use the **spark-submit** command to execute the Spark program. Here are the commands for running the program in Windows and Linux/macOS respectively.

Windows:

```
%SPARK_HOME%\bin\spark-submit --class "org.apache.spark.
examples.mllib.JavaRecommendationExample" --master lo
cal[*] target\spark-mllib-sample-1.0.jar
```

Linux/macOS:

```
$SPARK_HOME/bin/spark-submit --class "org.apache.spark.
examples.mllib.JavaRecommendationExample" --master lo
cal[*] target/spark-mllib-sample-1.0.jar
```

Monitoring the Spark MLlib application

We can monitor the Spark program status on the web console, which is available at http://localhost:4040/.

Let's look at some of the visualization tools that show the Spark machine-learning program statistics.

We can view the details of all jobs in the sample machine-learning program. Click on the Jobs tab on the web-console screen to navigate to the Spark Jobs webpage that shows these job details.

Figure 4.5 shows the status of the jobs from the sample program.

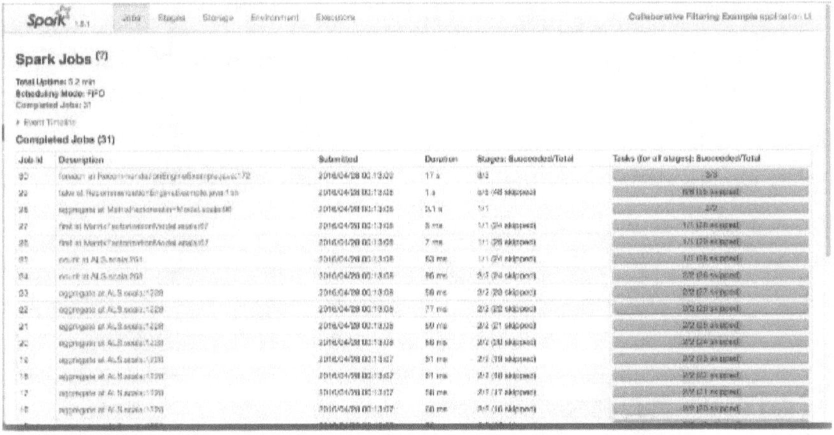

Figure 4.5. Spark jobs statistics for the machine-learning program.

The direct acyclic graph (DAG) shows the dependency graph of the different RDD operations we ran in the program. Figure 4.6 shows the screenshot of this visualization of the Spark machine-learning job.

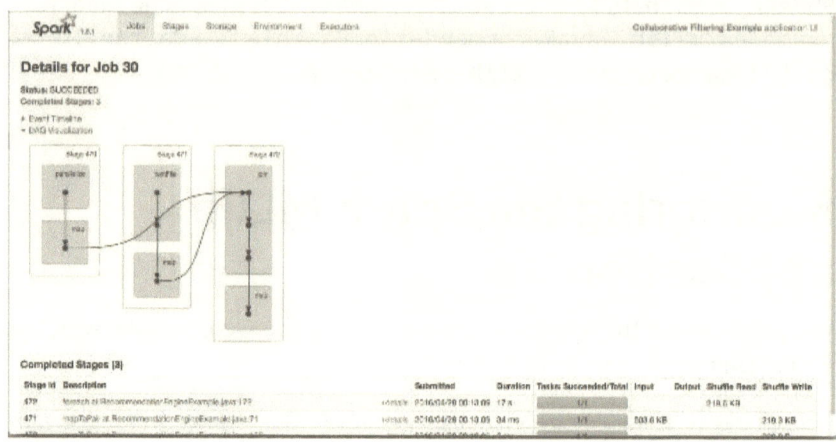

Figure 4.6. The DAG visualization of the Spark machine-learning program.

Conclusions

Spark MLlib is the machine-learning library from Apache Spark. It's used for implementing predictive analysis for business use cases like recommendation engines and fraud detection systems. In this section, we learned about how to use Spark MLlib to create a recommendation-engine application to predict the movies that a user might like.

Make sure to perform sufficient testing to assess the effectiveness as well as performance of different machine-learning techniques to find the best solution for each set of requirements and use cases.

References

- "Big Data Processing with Apache Spark — Part 1: Introduction"
- "Big Data Processing with Apache Spark — Part 2: Spark SQL"
- "Big Data Processing with Apache Spark — Part 3: Spark Streaming"
- Apache Spark homepage
- Spark MLlib homepage
- Spark MLlib: RDD-Based API guide
- Spark Summit machine-learning training exercise

PART
FIVE

Machine-Learning Data Pipelines

In the previous section, we looked at the Spark MLlib machine-learning library. This section focuses on the new machine-learning API from Spark, `spark.ml`, which is the recommended solution for big-data applications developed using data pipelines.

The `spark.ml` package provides a machine-learning API built on Data-Frames, which are becoming the core part of Spark SQL library. This package can be used to develop and manage the machine-learning pipelines. It also provides feature extractors, transformers, and selectors. It supports machine-learning techniques like classification, regression, and clustering. All of these are critical for developing machine-learning solutions.

We'll look at how we can use Apache Spark to perform exploratory data analysis (EDA), develop machine-learning pipelines, and use the APIs and algorithms available in the `spark.ml` package.

With support for building machine-learning data pipelines, Apache Spark is a great choice for building a unified product that combines ETL, batch analytics, real-time stream analysis, machine learning, graph processing, and visualizations.

Machine-learning data pipelines

Machine-learning pipelines are used for the creation, tuning, and inspection of machine-learning workflow programs. Machine-learning pipelines help us focus more on the big-data requirements and machine-learning tasks in our projects instead of spending time and effort on the infrastructure and distributed computing. They also help us with the exploratory stages of machine-learning problems, when we need to develop iterations of features and model combinations.

Machine-learning workflows often involve a sequence of processing and learning stages. A machine-learning data pipeline is a specified sequence of stages where each stage is either a transformer or an estimator component. These stages are executed in order, and the input data is transformed as it passes through each stage in the pipeline.

Machine-learning development frameworks need to support distributed computation as well as utilities to help with assembling the pipeline components. Other requirements for building data pipelines include fault tolerance, resource management, scalability, and maintainability.

Frameworks with machine-learning workflows also include utilities like model import/export, cross-validation to choose parameters, and aggregate data from multiple data sources. They provide data utilities like feature extraction, selection, and statistics. These frameworks support machine-learning-pipeline persistence to save and load machine-learning models and pipelines for future use.

The concept of machine-learning workflows and the composition of dataflow operators is becoming popular in several different systems. Big-data processing frameworks like scikit-learn and GraphLab use the concept of pipelines built into the system.

The process of a typical data value chain includes the following steps:

1. Discover
2. Ingest
3. Process
4. Persist
5. Integrate
6. Analyze
7. Expose

A machine-learning data pipeline follows a similar approach. The following table shows the different steps involved in a machine-learning-pipeline process.

Step #	Name	Description
ML1	Data ingestion	Loading the data from different data sources.
ML2	Data cleaning	Data is pre-processed to get it ready for the machine-learning data analysis.
ML3	Feature extraction	Also known as feature engineering, this step is about extracting the features from the datasets.
ML4	Model training	The machine-learning model is trained in the next step using the training datasets.

ML5	Model validation	Next, the machine-learning model is evaluated for effectiveness based on different prediction parameters. We also tune the model during the validation step. This step is used to pick the best model.
ML6	Model testing	The next step is to test the model before deploying it.
ML7	Model deployment	The final step is to deploy the selected model to execute in production environment.

Table 5.1. Machine-learning-pipeline process steps.

Figure 5.1 shows these steps.

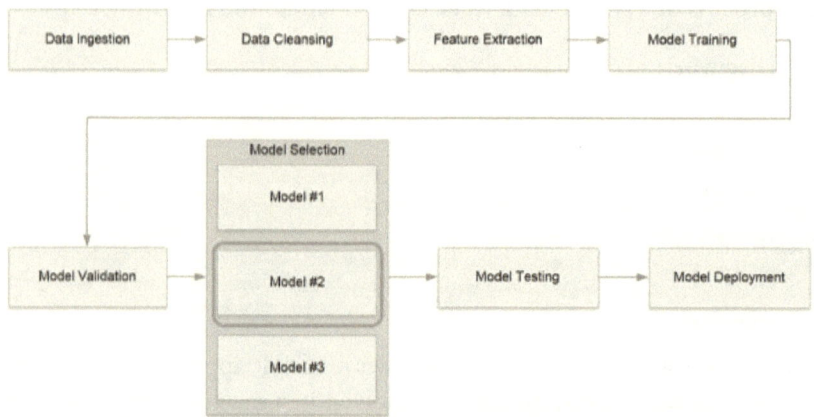

Figure 5.1. The flow diagram of a machine-learning data-pipeline process.

Let's look at each of these steps in more detail.

Data ingestion: The data we collect for a typical machine-learning-pipeline application can come from multiple data sources and can range from few hundred gigabytes to a terabyte. Also, one of the characteristics of big-data applications is ingesting data in different formats.

Data cleaning: Data cleaning is the first and critical step in the data-analysis pipeline. Also known as data cleansing, data scrubbing, or data wrangling, it's used to structure the data to facilitate data processing and predictive analysis. Depending on the quality of data coming into the system, 60-70% of time is spent in data cleaning to bring data to a format suitable for applying machine-learning models to it.

Data can have various quality issues like missing data or data elements with incorrect or irrelevant values. Data cleaning typically uses various approaches, including custom transformers.

Sparse or coarse-grained data is another challenge in data analysis. This is where many corner cases occur, and we have to apply data-cleaning techniques to make sure the data is of decent quality before feeding it to the data pipeline.

Data cleaning is usually an iterative process, as we more deeply understand the problem on each successive attempt and update the model iteratively. We can use data-wrangling tools like Trifacta, OpenRefine, and ActiveClean for data cleaning.

Feature extraction: In feature extraction (sometimes called feature engineering), we extract specific features from the raw data using techniques like feature hashing (hashing frequency of terms) and Word2vec. The results of this step are usually combined using an assembler component and are passed to next step in the process.

Model training: Model training in machine learning involves providing an algorithm and some training data that the model can learn from. The learning algorithm finds patterns in the training data and generates an output model.

Model validation: This step involves evaluating and tuning the machine-learning model to assess the accuracy of its predictions. As described in this Cloudera blog post, for binary classification models, the evaluation metric could be the area under the receiver-operating-characteristic (ROC) curve. A ROC curve illustrates the performance of a binary classifier system. It's created by plotting the true positive rate (TPR) against the false positive rate (FPR) at various threshold settings.

Model selection: Model selection uses data to choose parameters for transformers and estimators. This is a critical step in the machine-learning-pipeline process. Classes like `ParamGridBuilder` and `CrossValidator` provide APIs for selecting the machine-learning model.

Model deployment: Once we select the right model, we can deploy it and start feeding it new data, then receive the predictive analytical results. We can also deploy machine-learning models as web services.

The spark.ml package

Apache Spark introduced the machine-learning Pipelines API in version 1.2. It provides the API for developers to create and execute complex machine-learning workflows. The goal of the Pipelines API is to let users quickly and easily assemble and configure practical distributed machine-learning pipelines by standardizing the APIs for different machine-learning concepts. The Pipelines API is available in the `org.apache.spark.ml` package.

`spark.ml` also helps with combining multiple machine-learning algorithms into a single pipeline.

Spark's machine-learning API is divided into two packages: `spark.mllib` and `spark.ml`. The `spark.mllib` package contains the original API built on top of RDDs. The `spark.ml` package provides a higher-level API built on top of DataFrames for constructing machine-learning pipelines.

The MLlib library API that is based on RDDs is now in maintenance mode.

`spark.ml` is an important big-data analysis library in the Apache Spark ecosystem, as shown in Figure 5.2.

Spark Ecosystem with Spark Machine Learning Library

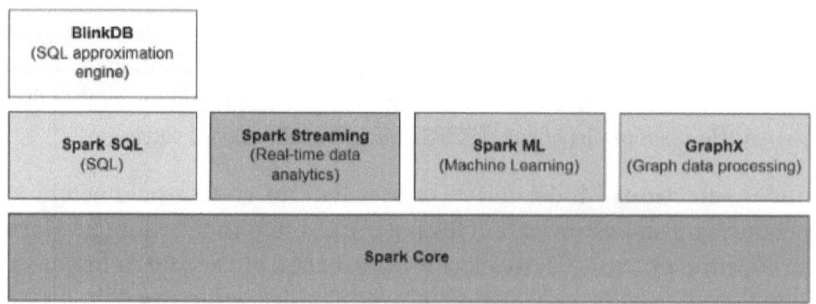

Figure 5.2. The Spark ecosystem with `spark.ml`.

Components of a machine-learning pipeline

A machine-learning pipeline that analyzes data consists of several components:

- datasets
- pipelines,
- pipeline stages (transformers and estimators),
- evaluators, and
- parameters (and `ParamMap`).

Let's take a quick look at where each of these components fits into the overall process.

Datasets: DataFrame is used to represent datasets in a machine-learning pipeline. It lets us store structured data in named columns. We can use the columns to store text, feature vectors, true labels, and predictions.

Pipelines: Machine-learning workflows are modeled as pipelines, which consist of a sequence of stages. Each stage transforms input data to produce output for succeeding stages. A pipeline chains multiple transformers and estimators together to specify a machine-learning workflow.

Pipeline stages: We define two kinds of stages: transformers and estimators. A transformer is an algorithm that can transform one DataFrame into another DataFrame (for example, a machine-learning model is a transformer that transforms a DataFrame with features into a DataFrame with predictions).

A transformer converts a DataFrame into another DataFrame while adding one or more features to it. For example, in the `spark.ml` package, OneHotEncoder transforms a column with a label index into a column of vectored features. Every transformer calls a `transform()` method to transform one DataFrame into another.

An estimator is an algorithm that learns from provided data. We use an estimator to train the model. The input to an estimator is a DataFrame and its output is a transformer. For example, a `LogisticRegression` estimator produces a `LogisticRegressionModel` transformer. Another example is k-means, which as an estimator accepts a training DataFrame and produces a k-means model that is a transformer.

Parameters: Machine-learning components use a common API for specifying parameters. An example of a parameter is the maximum number of iterations that the model should use.

The components of a data pipeline for a text-classification use case are shown in the following diagram.

Use cases

One of the use cases for machine-learning pipelines is text categorization. This use case typically includes the following steps:

1. Clean the text data.
2. Transform data into feature vectors.
3. Train the classification model.

In text categorization or classification, data-preprocessing steps like n-gram extraction and TF-IDF feature weighting are used before the training of a classification model (like SVM).

Text Classification Process Flow

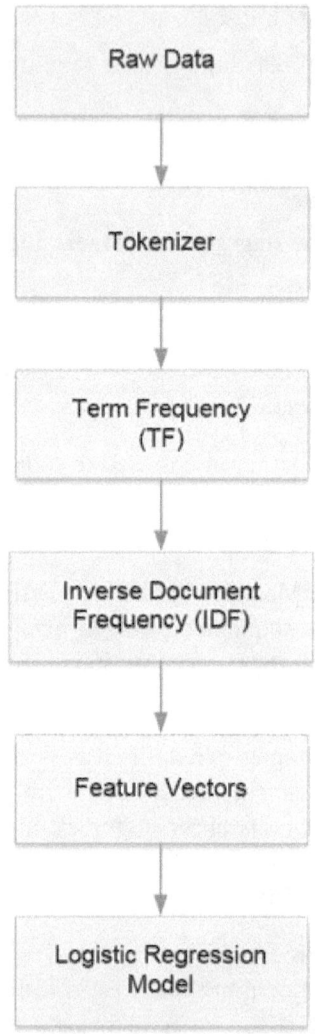

Figure 5.3. Data pipelines using `spark.ml`.

Another use case for a machine-learning pipeline is image classification as described in this article from AMPLab.

Other machine-learning use cases include fraud detection (using a classification model that is part of supervised learning) and user segmentation (using a clustering model that is part of unsupervised learning).

TF-IDF

TF-IDF, or "term frequency — inverse document frequency", is an information-retrieval algorithm that evaluates how important a word is to the collection of documents in which it appears.

If a word appears frequently, it's important. This term frequency (TF) is calculated as:

```
TF = (# of times word X appears in a document) /
(Total # of words in the document)
```

But if a word appears in many documents (like the words "the", "and", and "of" might), the algorithm decides that the word is not meaningful and lowers its score. This is the inverse document frequency.

Sample application

Let's look at a sample application to see how we can use the spark.ml package in a big-data processing system. We'll develop a document-classification application to identify spam content in the datasets provided to the application. The datasets are documents, e-mail messages, or other content received from external systems that can contain spam content.

We'll use the spam-detection example discussed in the "Building machine-learning apps with Spark" workshop at the 2016 Strata + Hadoop World conference to build our sample application.

The latest version of the code examples discussed in this section are available at the fol-lowing Github project:

https://github.com/spenchikala/big-data-processing-spark-mini-book

Use case

This use case is to analyze messages sent to our system. Some of these messages contain spam; the messages we get without any spam are called "ham" data. Our goal is to find the messages that contain spam using the `spark.ml` package API.

Algorithm

We'll use a logistic-regression algorithm in our machine-learning program. Logistic regression is a regression analysis model used to predict the probability of a binary response ("yes" or "no") based on one or more independent variables.

Solution details

Let's look at the details of the sample application and the steps we will be running as part of the `spark.ml` program.

For data ingestion, we'll load the datasets (text files) for the content that has the spam data as well as ham data that doesn't contain any spam.

In our sample application, we don't perform any specific data cleaning. We just aggregate all the data into a single DataFrame object.

We create an array object by randomly selecting data from both training and test datasets. In our example, we divide the datasets into one data object that will serve as training data (this contains 70% of the total data) and another that will serve as test data to gauge the application's predictive accuracy (30% of the total data).

Our machine-learning data pipeline includes four steps:

- Tokenizer,
- HashingTF,
- IDF, and
- LR.

We create a pipeline object and set the above stages in the pipeline. Then we create a logistic-regression model based on the training data.

Now, we can make predictions on the model using the test data.

Figure 5.4 shows the architecture of the sample application.

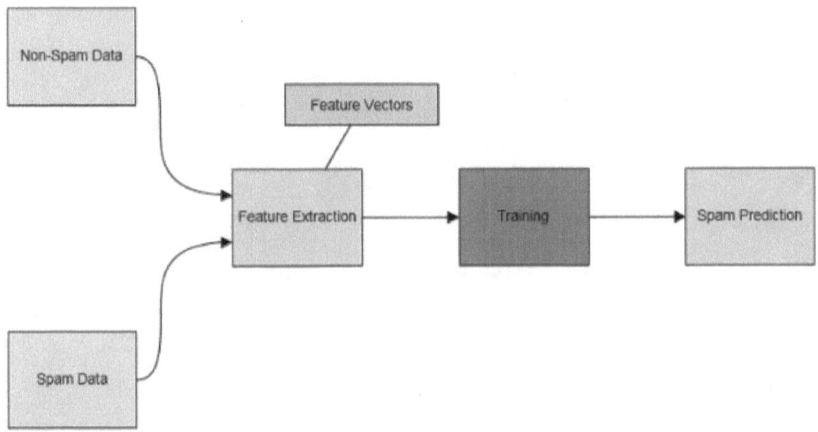

Figure 5.4. Architecture of the data-classification application.

Technologies

We'll use the following technologies in implementing the machine-learning-pipeline solution.

Technology	Version
Apache Spark	2.2.0
JDK	8
Maven	3.3

Table 5.2. Technologies and tools used in our machine-learning sample application.

A spark.ml program

The sample machine-learning code from the workshop example is written in the Scala programming language and we can run the program using the Spark shell console.

Step 1: Create a custom class to store the details of spam content.

```
case class SpamDocument(file: String, text: String,
label:
Double)
```

Step 2: Initialize SQLContext and import the implicits methods to convert Scala objects into DataFrames. Then load the datasets from the specified directory where the files are located, which returns the RDD objects. Create DataFrame objects from the RDDs for both datasets.

```
val sqlContext = new SQLContext(sc)
import sqlContext.implicits._

//
// Load the data files with spam
//
val rddSData = sc.wholeTextFiles("SPAM_DATA_FILE_DIR",
1)
val dfSData = rddSData.map(d => SpamDocument(d._1, d._2,
1)).toDF()
dfSData.show()

//
// Load the data files with no spam
//
val rddNSData = sc.wholeTextFiles("NO_SPAM_DATA_FILE_
DIR",
1)
val dfNSData = rddNSData.map(d => SpamDocument(d._1,
d._2, 0)).toDF()
dfNSData.show()
```

Step 3: Now, aggregate the datasets and split the 70% of the data into a training dataset and 30% into a test dataset.

```
//
// Aggregate both data frames
//
val dfAllData = dfSData.unionAll(dfNSData)
dfAllData.show()

//
// Split the data into 70% training data and 30% test
data
//
val Array(trainingData, testData) =
dfAllData.randomSplit(Array(0.7, 0.3))
```

Step 4: We now can configure the machine-learning data pipeline, which includes creating the components listed earlier: Tokenizer, HashingTF, and IDF. Then create the regression model, in this case LogisticRegression, using the training data.

```
//
// Configure the ML data pipeline
//

//
// Create the Tokenizer step
//
val tokenizer = new Tokenizer()
  .setInputCol("text")
  .setOutputCol("words")

//
// Create the TF and IDF steps
//
val hashingTF = new HashingTF()
  .setInputCol(tokenizer.getOutputCol)
  .setOutputCol("rawFeatures")

val idf = new
IDF().setInputCol("rawFeatures").setOutputCol
("features")
```

```
//
// Create the Logistic Regression step
//
val lr = new LogisticRegression()
  .setMaxIter(5)
lr.setLabelCol("label")
lr.setFeaturesCol("features")

//
// Create the pipeline
//
val pipeline = new Pipeline()
  .setStages(Array(tokenizer, hashingTF, idf, lr))

val lrModel = pipeline.fit(trainingData)
println(lrModel.toString())
```

Step 5: Finally, we can call the transform method in the logistic-regression model to make the predictions on the test data.

```
//
// Make predictions.
//
val predictions = lrModel.transform(testData)

//
// Display prediction results
//
predictions.select("file", "text", "label", "features",
"prediction").show(300)
```

Conclusions

The Spark machine-learning library is one of the critical libraries in the Apache Spark framework. It's used for implementing data pipelines. In this section, we learned about the spark.ml package API and how to use it in a text-classification use case.

References

- "Big Data Processing with Apache Spark — Part 1: Introduction"
- "Big Data Processing with Apache Spark — Part 2: Spark SQL"
- "Big Data Processing with Apache Spark — Part 3: Spark Streaming"
- "Big Data Processing with Apache Spark — Part 4: Spark Machine Learning"
- Apache Spark homepage
- Spark MLlib homepage
- Spark Machine Learning Library (MLlib) Guide
- "Building machine-learning apps with Spark" workshop exercise

PART SIX

Graph Data Analytics
with Spark GraphX

Big data comes in different shapes and sizes. It can be batch data that needs to be processed offline — processing a large set of records and generating the results and insights at a later time. Or the data can be real-time streams that need to be processed on the fly for almost instantaneous data insights.

We have seen how Apache Spark can be used to process batch data (Spark Core) as well as real-time data (Spark Streaming).

Sometimes, the data we need to deal with is connected in nature. For example, in a social-media application, we have entities like users, articles, likes, etc. that we need to manage and process as a single logical unit of data. This type of data is called graph data and requires different analytical techniques and approaches from traditional data processing.

This section will focus on how to process graph data and Spark's GraphX graph data-analysis library.

First, let's look at what graph data is and why it's critical to process this type of data in enterprise big-data applications.

Graph data

There are three different topics to cover when we discuss graph-data-related technologies:

- graph databases,
- graph data analysis, and
- graph data visualization.

Let's discuss these topics briefly to learn how they differ and how they complement each other to help us develop a comprehensive graph-based big-data processing and analysis architecture.

Graph databases

Unlike traditional data models, graph data models have as core elements data entities as well as the relationships between those entities. When working on graph data, we are interested in the entities and the connections between them.

For example, if we are working on a social-network application, we would be interested in the details of a particular user (let's say John) but we would also want to model, store, and retrieve any associations between this user and other users in the network. Examples of these associations are "John is a friend of Mike" or "John read the book written by Bob."

It's important to remember the real-world graph data we use in applications is dynamic in nature and changes over time.

Graph databases allow us to uncover patterns that are usually difficult to detect using traditional data models and analytic approaches.

Available graph databases include Neo4j, DataStax Enterprise Graph, AllegroGraph, InfiniteGraph, and OrientDB.

Graph data modeling

Graph data modeling includes defining the nodes (also known as vertices), the relationships (also known as edges), and the labels for those nodes and relationships.

Graph databases are based on what Jim Webber of Neo Technologies calls "query-driven modeling", which means the data model is open to domain experts rather than only database specialists, and it supports team collaboration for modeling and evolution.

Graph databases like Neo4J provide a query language (Cypher in the case of Neo4j) to manage the graph data stored in the database.

Graph data processing

Graph data processing mainly includes graph traversal to find specific nodes in the graph dataset that match the specified patterns and then locating the associated nodes and relationships in the data so we can see the connection patterns among different entities.

The data processing pipeline typically includes the following steps:

- pre-processing of data (which includes loading, transformation, and filtering),
- graph creation,
- analysis, and
- post-processing.

A typical graph analysis tool should provide the flexibility to work with both graphs and collections so that we can combine data-analysis tasks like ETL, exploratory analysis, and iterative graph computation within a single system without having to use several different frameworks and tools.

There are several frameworks that we can use to process graph data and run predictive analysis on the data. These include Spark GraphX, Apache Flink's Gelly, and GraphLab Create.

In this section, we'll focus on Spark GraphX for analyzing the graph data.

There are also several different graph generators, as noted in the Gelly documentation, like cycle graph, grid graph, hypercube graph, path graph, and star graph.

Graph data visualization

Once we start storing connected data in a graph database and analyze this graph data, we need tools to visualize the patterns in the relationships among data entities. Without visualization tools, data-analysis efforts are not complete.

Graph data visualization tools include D3.js, Linkurious, and GraphLab Canvas.

Graph use cases

There are a variety of use cases for which graph databases are better fit to manage the data than solutions like relational databases or other NoSQL data stores. Some of these use cases include the following.

Recommendations and personalization: Graph data analysis can be used to generate recommendation and personalization models for customers and the insights found in the data analysis can influence key decisions. This helps a company persuade customers to purchase its product. This analysis also helps with marketing strategy and to assess customer-service behavior.

Fraud detection: Graph data solutions also help reveal fraudulent transactions in a payment-processing application, based on connected data that include entities like users, products, transactions, and events. This phData blog post describes a test application that uses Spark GraphX for fraud detection in phone communication using the PageRank algorithm on metadata.

Topic modeling: This includes techniques that cluster documents and extract topical representations from the data in those documents.

Community detection: Alibaba.com's website uses graph-data-analysis techniques like community detection to solve e-commerce problems.

Flight performance: Other use cases, as discussed in this Databricks blog post, analyze flight-performance data organized in graph structures to reveal statistics like airport ranking, on-time performance, and shortest paths between cities.

Shortest distance: Discovering the shortest distances and paths is also useful in social-network applications. This can be used to measure the relevance of a particular user in the network. Users with smaller shortest distances are more relevant than users farther away.

Spark GraphX

GraphX is Apache Spark's API for graphs and graph-parallel computation. It extends the Spark RDD by introducing a new graph abstraction: a directed multigraph with properties attached to each vertex and edge.

The GraphX library provides graph operators like `subgraph`, `joinVertices`, and `aggregateMessages` to transform the graph data. It provides several ways to build a graph from a collection of vertices and edges in an RDD or on disk. GraphX also includes a number of graph algorithms and builders to use to perform graph analysis. We'll discuss graph algorithms later in this section.

Figure 6.1 shows where GraphX fits in the Apache Spark ecosystem.

Apache Spark Ecosystem with Spark GraphX Library

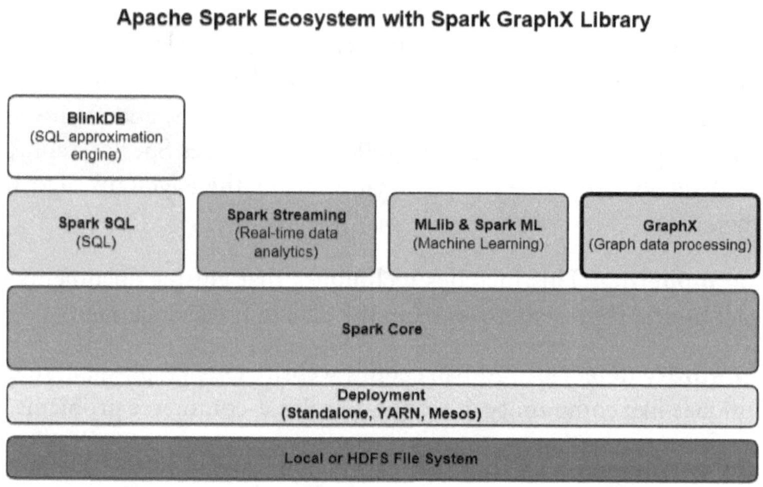

Figure 6.1. The Spark ecosystem and GraphX library.

GraphX makes it easier to run analysis on graph data with built-in operators and algorithms. It also allows us to cache and un-cache the graph data to avoid re-computation when we need to call a graph multiple times.

Some of the graph operators available in GraphX are listed in Table 6.1.

Operator Type	Operators	Description
Basic operators	numEdges numVertices inDegrees outDegrees degrees	Collection of operators that take the user-defined functions and produce new graphs.

Property operators	`mapVertices` `mapEdges` `mapTriplets`	These property graph operators result in a new graph with the vertex or edge properties modified by the user-defined function. They are often used to initialize the graph for a computation or to filter unnecessary properties.
Structural operators	`reverse` `subgraph` `mask` `groupEdges`	These operators are used to filter the main graph object to remove data we are not interested in.
Join operators	`joinVertices` `outerJoinVertices`	Used to join data from external data sources with the graph in the context.

Table 6.1. Spark GraphX's graph operators.

We'll look at these operators in detail in the "Sample application" section, when we run GraphX algorithms on different social-network datasets.

GraphFrames

GraphFrames, a new addition to the Spark graph data-processing tool-set, integrates features like pattern matching and graph algorithms with Spark SQL. Vertices and edges are represented as DataFrames instead of RDD objects.

GraphFrames simplify the graph-data-analysis pipeline and optimize the queries across both graph and relational data. It provides some advantages over RDD-based graph data processing:

• It has support for Python and Java in addition to Scala APIs, letting us use GraphX algorithms in all three languages.

- It has advanced query capability using Spark SQL and DataFrames. The graph-aware query planner uses materialized views to improve query performance.
- We can also save and load graphs in formats like Parquet, JSON, and CSV.

GraphFrames are available as an add-on component to GraphX from the Spark Packages website. This Cloudera blog post shows how to use GraphFrames to calculate the PageRank for each node in a graph dataset.

Graph analytics algorithms

Graph algorithms help with executing the analysis on graph datasets without having to write our own implementations of those algorithms. Below is a list of algorithms that help with finding patterns in graphs:

- PageRank,
- connected components,
- label propagation,
- SVD++,
- strongly connected components,
- triangle count,
- single-source shortest paths, and
- community detection.

Spark GraphX comes with a set of pre-built graph algorithms to help with graph data processing and analysis. These algorithms are available in the `org.apache.spark.graphx.lib` package. It's as simple as calling these algorithms as methods in a `Graph` class.

Figure 6.2 shows how the different graph algorithms are built on top of the base GraphX API.

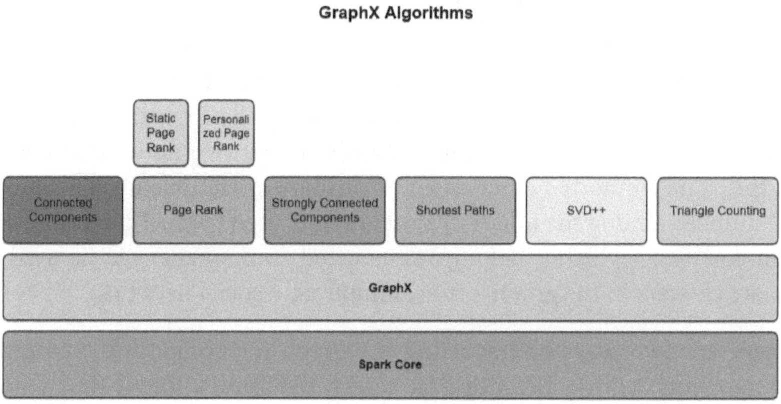

Figure 6.2. Graph algorithms in the Spark GraphX library.

Let's look more deeply into the PageRank, connected components, and triangle-counting algorithms.

PageRank

The PageRank algorithm is used to determine the relative importance of an object inside a graph dataset. It measures the importance of each node in a graph, assuming an edge from another node to this node represents an endorsement.

Google's search engine is a classic example of PageRank. Google uses PageRank to count how many other webpages link to a target webpage and uses the result as one measure in determining the importance of that target webpage.

Another example is a social network like Twitter. A Twitter user followed by a lot of users has a higher PageRank than users who don't have as many followers.

GraphX provides two implementations of PageRank: static and dynamic. Static PageRank runs for a fixed number of iterations to generate PageRank values for a given set of nodes in a graph dataset. Dynamic PageRank, on the other hand, runs until PageRank values converge based on a pre-defined tolerance value.

Connected components

A connected component in a graph is defined as subgraph of nodes (or vertices) that connect to each other and no other nodes in the larger main graph. A connected component is isolated from all other connected components in the main graph. This means that any two nodes that belong to the same connected component must share a relationship. The lowest ID number among the nodes in a subgraph is used to label the connected component to which it belongs. Connected components can be used to create clusters in the graph — for example, in a social network.

There are two ways of traversing the graph for computing connected components: with a breadth-first search (BFS) or a depth-first search (DFS).

There is another algorithm called strongly connected components (SCC) in graph data processing. If all nodes in a graph are reachable from every other node, then we consider the graph to be strongly connected.

Triangle counting

Triangle counting is a community-detection graph algorithm that determines the number of triangles passing through each vertex in the graph dataset. As the name implies, a triangle is a three-node subgraph with each node connected to the other two. This algorithm returns a graph object and we extract vertices from this triangle-counting graph.

Triangle counting is used heavily in social-network analysis. It provides a measure of clustering in the graph data, which is useful for finding communities and measuring the cohesiveness of local communities in social networks like LinkedIn or Facebook. The clustering coefficient, an important metric in social networks, shows how tightly a community connects or clusters around one of its nodes.

Note that PageRank is a measure of relevancy whereas triangle count is a measure of clustering.

Other use cases for the triangle-counting algorithm are spam detection and link recommendations.

Triangle counting is a message-heavy and computationally expensive algorithm compared to other graph algorithms so run the Spark program on a decent hardware infrastructure.

Sample application

We have seen in this section what graph data is and why graph analysis is an important part of big data-processing projects. Let's now look at a sample application that uses some of the graph algorithms.

We'll use datasets from the social networks Facebook, LiveJournal, and YouTube. All of these produce connected data and are excellent resources for graph-data-analysis programs.

The examples we use here are based on the GraphX examples from a comparison of the Dato and GraphX graph processing tools.

The latest version of the code examples discussed in this section are available at the fol-lowing Github project:

https://github.com/spenchikala/big-data-processing-spark-mini-book

Use cases

The main goal of the use cases in our sample application is to determine graph data statistics such as:

- the popularity of different users in the social network (PageRank),
- clusters of users based on how users connect in the social network (connected components), and
- community detection and cohesiveness of the communities of users in the social network (triangle counting).

Datasets

In our code examples, we will run a few different datasets through Spark GraphX programs. These datasets are available from the Stanford Network Analysis Project (SNAP) website. To use these datasets in our application, download them and copy them to a data folder in the sample application's main directory.

Algorithms

We'll use the following algorithms in our sample application:

- PageRank on YouTube data,
- connected components on LiveJournal data, and
- triangle counting on Facebook data.

The following table shows the use cases, datasets, and algorithms used in the graph-data processing programs.

Use Case	Dataset Source	Link	File Name	Rename File As
PageRank	YouTube	https://snap.stanford. edu/data/com-Youtube. html	com-youtube. ungraph.txt	page-rank-yt-data.txt
Connected components	Live Journal	https://snap.stanford. edu/data/com-LiveJournal.html	com-lj. ungraph.txt	connected-components-lj-data.txt
Triangle count	Facebook	https://snap.stanford. edu/data/egonets-Facebook.html	facebook_combined.txt	triangle-count-fb-data.txt

Table 6.2: Datasets and algorithms used in the Spark GraphX sample application.

Technologies

We'll use the following technologies in the graph-analysis sample application.

Technology	Apache Spark	Scala	JDK	Maven
Version	2.2	2.11	8	33

Table 6.3. Technologies and tools used in the sample application.

Code example

We'll write the Spark GraphX code using the Scala programming language. We'll use the Spark shell command-line tool to run these programs. This is the fastest way to verify the results of the program. We need no additional code compilation or build steps.

These programs will be available as a .zip file on the book website for you to download and try out in your own development environment.

Let's look at the details of each of the sample GraphX programs.

First, we will run PageRank on the YouTube social-network data. This dataset includes the ground-truth communities, which are basically user-defined groups that other users can join.

PageRank:

```
import org.apache.spark._
import org.apache.spark.graphx._
import org.apache.spark.rdd.RDD
import java.util.Calendar

// Load the edges as a graph
val graph = GraphLoader.edgeListFile(sc, "data/page-
rank-yt-data.txt")
// Get the graph details like edges, vertices etc.

val vertexCount = graph.numVertices

val vertices = graph.vertices
vertices.count()

val edgeCount = graph.numEdges

val edges = graph.edges
edges.count()

val triplets = graph.triplets
// Following method call to collect() takes long time to
run
// triplets.collect()
triplets.count()
```

```
triplets.take(5)

val inDegrees = graph.inDegrees
inDegrees.collect()

val outDegrees = graph.outDegrees
outDegrees.collect()

val degrees = graph.degrees
degrees.collect()

// Number of iterations as the argument
val staticPageRank = graph.staticPageRank(10)
staticPageRank.vertices.collect()

Calendar.getInstance().getTime()
val pageRank = graph.pageRank(0.001).vertices
Calendar.getInstance().getTime()

// Print top 5 items from the result
println(pageRank.top(5).mkString("\n"))
```

Let's now look at the code that runs connected components on LiveJournal's social-network data. This dataset includes registered users who have submitted individual and group blog posts. The LiveJournal website also allows users to identify other users as friends.

Connected components:

```
import org.apache.spark._
import org.apache.spark.graphx._
import org.apache.spark.rdd.RDD
import java.util.Calendar

// Connected Components
val graph = GraphLoader.edgeListFile(sc, "data/connect
ed-components-lj-data.txt")

Calendar.getInstance().getTime()
val cc = graph.connectedComponents()
Calendar.getInstance().getTime()

cc.vertices.collect()
```

```
// Print top 5 items from the result
println(cc.vertices.take(5).mkString("\n"))

val scc = graph.stronglyConnectedComponents()
scc.vertices.collect()
```

Finally, this Spark program, in Scala, performs triangle counting on Facebook's social-circles data. The dataset includes the lists of Facebook friends with user profiles, circles, and ego networks.

Triangle counting:

```
import org.apache.spark.SparkContext
import org.apache.spark.SparkContext._
import org.apache.spark.graphx._
import org.apache.spark.rdd.RDD

val graph = GraphLoader.edgeListFile(sc,"data/trian
gle-count-fb-data.txt")

println("Number of vertices : " + graph.vertices.
count())
println("Number of edges : " + graph.edges.count())

graph.vertices.foreach(v => println(v))

val tc = graph.triangleCount()

tc.vertices.collect

println("tc: " + tc.vertices.take(5).mkString("\n"));

// println("Triangle counts: " + graph.connected
Components.triangleCount().vertices.collect().mk
String("\n"));

println("Triangle counts: " + graph.connectedComponents.
triangleCount().vertices.top(5).mkString("\n"));

val sum = tc.vertices.map(a => a._2).reduce((a, b) => a
+ b)
```

Conclusions

With the increasing growth of connected data in commercial organizations, government agencies, and social-media companies, graph data processing and analysis are only going to become more critical in predictive analysis and recommendation-engine solutions as they provide insights and service for employees, customers, and users.

Spark GraphX is a superb choice for graph data processing. It provides a unified data-processing algorithm and solution toolset for delivering valuable insight and prediction models on the connected data generated by business processes in organizations.

As we have seen, the Apache Spark framework provides the necessary libraries, utilities, and tools for unified big-data processing-application architectures. Whether we need to process the data in real time or in a batch mode or if the dataset has connections and relationships, Spark makes working with different types of data easier. We no longer need to depend on several different frameworks to process and analyze the different types of data generated in a typical organization.

If we're looking for a big-data solution for applications in our organizations or we're interested in getting into big data and data science, Spark is an excellent framework to learn and use in applications.

References

- "Big Data Processing with Apache Spark — Part 1: Introduction"
- "Big Data Processing with Apache Spark — Part 2: Spark SQL"
- "Big Data Processing with Apache Spark — Part 3: Spark Streaming"
- "Big Data Processing with Apache Spark — Part 4: Spark Machine Learning"

- "Big Data Processing with Apache Spark — Part 5: Spark ML Data Pipelines"
- Apache Spark homepage
- Apache Spark GraphX homepage
- GraphX Programming Guide
- Spark GraphX in Action (Manning Publications)
- "Facebook's Comparison of Apache Giraph and Spark GraphX for Graph Data Processing"
- Databricks blog post on GraphFrames

PART
SEVEN

Emerging Trends
in Data Science

Data science and big data are seeing exponential growth in popularity and technologies. Because of the increased presence and usage of Internet of Things (IoT) devices, IoT-related data is also growing by leaps and bounds.

New technologies like deep learning, natural-language processing (NLP), virtual reality (VR), augmented reality (AR), and autonomous-vehicle technology (AVT or self-driving cars) are getting a lot of attention recently. Other areas also getting more focus are artificial intelligence (AI), computer vision, and image processing.

In this last section of the book, we are going to briefly discuss some of these technologies.

AI is a broad field of science that includes machine learning, which includes deep-learning technologies.

Deep learning

Deep learning uses a cascade of many layers of non-linear processing units for feature extraction and transformation. Each successive layer uses the output from the previous layer as input. The algorithms may be supervised or unsupervised and applications include pattern analysis (unsupervised) and classification (supervised).

Deep learning can be used for computer vision, speech recognition, and NLP.

Some deep learning technologies include TensorFlow (from Google), Theano, Caffe, MXNet (from Apache), and DeepLearning4J.

Computer vision

Computer vision is used to process and analyze images and to detect objects in those images. It is used to develop 3-D models for predictive analysis, which are used in applications for autonomous vehicles.

Frameworks like OpenCV and Microsoft's Computer Vision API can be used in image analysis to return visual content in the images. It can also help with identifying image types and color schemes in pictures.

Natural-language processing

NLP algorithms allow computer programs to process and understand natural-language text. NLP can be applied in use cases such as text similarity, sentiment analysis, automatic question answering, relationship extraction, and topic segmentation.

NLP frameworks include:

- Natural Language Toolkit (NLTK) (based on Python),
- Stanford CoreNLP, and
- Apache OpenNLP.

Augmented reality

Augmented reality (AR) is a view (direct or indirect) of the actual physical environment augmented and superimposed by additional sensory input such as audio, video, and device specifications.

Unlike VR technology, which provides an entirely virtual environment, AR uses the existing natural environment as background for the virtual information that it lays on top of it. AR technologies lie in the middle of the mixed-reality spectrum, between the real and virtual worlds.

AR is useful in various industries like manufacturing, health care, and the military, as well as our everyday lives.

Conversational AI

Conversational AI is a technology of human/computer interaction (HCI). It includes developing chatbots or virtual assistants, computer programs that can interact with humans in a conversational way using text or voice as input. Many products have been released in this space in recent years, including Amazon's Lex and Polly technologies and Alexa, Google Home, Apple's HomePod and Siri, and Microsoft's Bot Framework.

Suggestions for Further Reading

The InfoQ eMag Getting a Handle on Data Science provides a good overview of the subject in general.

Our Introduction to Machine Learning eMag provides an introduction to some powerful but generally applicable techniques in machine learning. These include deep learning but also more traditional methods that are often all the modern business needs.

For more information related to data science, check out the Data Science section of the InfoQ website.

Other resources for data science and big data include Data Science Central and the Strata Data Conference, which offers valuable conference sessions and workshops on big data in general and Apache Spark in particular.

Conference events like Spark Summit offer excellent learning material on Spark and related big-data technologies with video presentations and full training classes recorded at the events.

Also, keep an eye on the upcoming QCon.ai conference to learn about the design patterns, best practices, and use cases for applying artificial intelligence and machine Learning in your applications.

www.ingramcontent.com/pod-product-compliance
Lightning Source LLC
Chambersburg PA
CBHW022106170526
45157CB00004B/1502